Liberty for All? 1820–1860

TEACHING GUIDE FOR THE THIRD EDITION

For Elementary School Classes

Oxford University Press
Oxford   New York
Auckland   Bangkok   Buenos Aires
Cape Town   Chennai   Dar es Salaam   Delhi   Hong Kong   Istanbul
Karachi   Kolkata   Kuala Lumpur   Madrid   Melbourne   Mexico City   Mumbai
Nairobi   São Paulo   Shanghai   Singapore   Taipei   Tokyo   Toronto

and an associated company
Berlin

Copyright © 2003 by Oxford University Press, Inc.

Published by Oxford University Press, Inc.
198 Madison Avenue, New York, New York 10016
Oxford is a registered trademark of Oxford University Press

All rights reserved. No part of this publication may be reproduced, stored in a retrieval system, or transmitted in any form or by any means, electronic, mechanical, photocopying, recording, or otherwise, without the prior permission of Oxford University Press.

ISBN 978-0-19-976738-0

Writer: Karen Edwards
Editor: Rosely Himmelstein
Editorial Consultant: Susan Buckley

Printed in the United States of America on acid-free paper

CONTENTS

Note from the Author   4
About This Teaching Guide   5
Literacy and *A History of US*   8
Assessment and *A History of US*   9
Historical Overview   10

Teaching Strategies for Book Five
    Part 1: Heading Westward (Chapters 1-7)   12
    Part 2: Extending Boundaries (Chapters 8-12)   21
    Part 3: Reaching Across Land and Sea (Chapters 13-17)   28
    Part 4: Pursuing Progress (Chapters 18-20)   35
    Part 5: Seeking Perfection (Chapters 21-26)   40
    Part 6: Creating a National Identity (Chapters 27-31)   48
    Part 7: Challenging Slavery (Chapters 32-38)   55

Part Check-Ups   64
Resources   71
Answer Key   86

NOTE FROM THE AUTHOR

Dear Teacher,

Every writer of history has to make decisions. Most of those decisions are about what to leave out. It would take libraries and libraries of books to include all of America's history (and there would still be things left out).

So there are all kinds of stories about America (and its heroes and villains and ordinary people) that are not in this book. I see that as an opportunity for you and your students. Tell them the author is upset about what she had to omit. Have them do their own chapters of *A History of US*. Maybe you can do a class volume. Consider focusing on family stories: what can each of your students find out about his or her ancestors? Or maybe you'll want to do a book about your community with chapters on people and organizations and past events.

I have fun tracking down stories; I think you and your students will, too. (Yes, I hope you'll become a student with them.) Writing history is a lot like being a detective or a newspaper reporter. It involves searching for information, digesting it, and then using it. There are hardly any better skills for this Information Age of ours.

You and your students might want to find out more about the early presidents or Lewis and Clark or early 19th-century inventors. Or about Americans not even mentioned in these books. Good writers look for details. Check paintings and photographs. What does your subject look like? How did he or she dress? What was daily life like for that person?

You might want to produce the work in comic book form, or write it as a play, or create a ballad. The big idea here is to "do" history, as you might do art or music. At its best, it's a creative activity.

But the big reason I wrote these books was to teach reading and, when it comes to critical reading, history shines. Few subjects give you real events and real people to discuss and analyze. Literacy exercises and paragraph analysis may help some students, but there is nothing like reading a whole book—tracing its ideas from chapter to chapter, and then talking about the ideas—to make a mind work.

This learning guide has words to study and maps to look at and questions to answer. You may want your students to do all the activities, or you may want them to do just a few. Some activities are for those who want to go beyond the text.

Will all this help students pass standardized tests? You bet. Just to be sure, though, I have added some pages with names and dates that you may ask students to memorize.

But there are things in history more important than memorized dates. History is a thinking subject, and you have Information Age kids as your charge. Doing history means reading, researching, finding information, and making connections. If you want to stretch young minds, history will make it happen.

Joy Hakim

ABOUT THIS TEACHING GUIDE

A History of US is the story of what happened in the United States to the people who live here—both before and after the country got its name. In *Liberty for All?*, students will learn what happened between 1820 and 1860. This teaching guide, containing strategies and assessment suggestions as well as a range of activities for enrichment and extension, was prepared to help you guide your students through the book.

FOCUSING ON FREEDOM

The cornerstone of American history is Freedom. It is the idea that pulsates throughout *A History of US*: the hunger for freedom, the fight for freedom, the legislating of freedom, the protection of freedom, the defense of freedom. As you teach this volume of *A History of US*, students will learn how the accomplishments of people, the force of ideas, and the outcome of events are all linked in this nation's great story of Freedom.

A lot happens: sad, exhilarating, unexpected, disappointing, terrible, puzzling, inspiring things. And many people are involved: the wise, the misguided, the brave, the reckless, the patient, the bullies, the compromisers. It's a grand and sweeping story.

May you and your students enjoy it together.

THE TEACHING UNITS

Each book of *A History of US* has been divided into units of study that we call Parts. Each Part consists of chapters that have a common focus. The Teaching Guide provides strategies and activities that you can use to teach each Part.

- **Part 1: Heading Westward (Chapters 1-7)** focuses on westward expansion.

- **Part 2: Extending Boundaries (Chapters 8-12)** focuses on manifest destiny and conflicts with Mexico over acquisition of Texas and California.

- **Part 3: Reaching Across Land and Sea (Chapters 13-17)** focuses on networks of transportation and communication that linked East to West.

- **Part 4: Pursuing Progress (Chapters 18-20)** focuses on progress in the eastern cities.

- **Part 5: Seeking Perfection (Chapters 21-26)** focuses on education and the expansion of human rights.

- **Part 6: Creating a National Identity (Chapters 27-31)** focuses on cultural achievements in literature, art, and philosophy.

- **Part 7: Challenging Slavery (Chapters 32-38)** focuses on the struggles over slavery before the Civil War period.

ORGANIZING INFORMATION

The history of the United States is rich, busy, and populated. You can help your students organize information and reinforce learning by frequently asking these questions:

- What were the major events?
- Who were the significant people?
- What were the important ideas?

☑ **Question Chart** In every lesson plan, you will see a reference to the Question Chart (Resource 1, TG page 71), on which students may record their answers to these questions as they progress through the book.

THE BIG THEMES

Underlying the events and people and ideas that enliven this series are certain themes—themes that run through human experience and help us make sense of the past.

Among these themes are Justice, Conflict, Independence, Change, Diversity, Adaptation, Growth, and Power. You may wish to post these themes on the walls of your classroom and refer to them at appropriate times. They may also stir students' thinking throughout the course of their study.

Book 5 of *A History of US* focuses on three Big Themes: **Expansion, Conflict,** and **Human Rights.** These themes—and how they relate to this nation's quest for and preservation of freedom—provide the conceptual framework of *Liberty for All?*

Factors that contributed to U.S. expansion during this period are:

- increased migration of people westward.
- the influence of the concept of manifest destiny.
- the acquisition of Texas and California.
- the discovery of gold in California.
- improved transportation and communication.

Among the major conflicts in this period are:

- the conflict between the United States and Mexico.
- the conflict over the admission of Texas to the Union.
- the conflict between settlers and Native Americans in the Northwest.
- the growing conflict between the North and the South over the issue of slavery.

Among the human rights issues in this period are:

- the persecution of the Mormons.
- the beginning of the demand for the education and rights of women.
- the issue of child labor and "wage slaves" in factories.
- increased awareness of the lack of rights among enslaved people.

TEACHING STRATEGIES

The Teaching Strategies in this guide are organized in the following manner:

Introducing the Part lays out goals for teaching, sets up a relationship between the Part and the major themes, and seeks to stimulate students' interest as they begin to read the text.

Chapter Lesson Plans are designed to provide you with the flexibility that your individual schedule, interests, and students' abilities may require. You may choose from the following categories:

- **Ask:** straightforward questions to elicit from your students responses that demonstrate their recall and understanding of the text.
- **Discuss:** critical thinking questions to stimulate classroom and/or small-group discussions.
- **Write:** topics for classroom or homework assignment, allowing students to express their comprehension or impressions of the chapter's events, ideas, or people.
- **Ponder:** questions that give students the opportunity to reflect on the thematic material of the chapter, often relating it to their own lives.
- **Literacy Links:** *Words to Discuss,* exploring the chapter's significant vocabulary words or terms, and *Reading Skills* designed to help students develop reading skills, especially for reading nonfiction.
- **Skills Connection:** chapter-related activities to strengthen geography skills, chart/graph skills, study skills, and cross-curricula skills.
- **Meeting Individual Needs:** activities that address the needs of students with differing learning abilities.

Which of these categories will be suitable for your students on any particular day? How many items will be useful to engage your class—or a particular student? The lesson plans have been structured with the belief that *you* are the best person to make these decisions.

Summarizing the Part provides guidance for synthesizing the Part's Big Themes. This guidance consists of a series of questions—which you can use for assessment or discussion—that enable students to deepen their understanding of how the events, ideas, trends, and personalities of the Part reflect common themes. The Part Summary also provides additional Projects and Activities.

PART CHECK-UPS

The reproducible Check-Ups review the content of each Part.

RESOURCES

The Resources are reproducible blackline masters. They cover social studies skills (including maps, graphic organizers, tables, primary sources, and other enrichment materials), critical thinking skills, and reading comprehension skills.

LITERACY AND *A HISTORY OF US*

In our Information Age, reading is an essential survival skill. So what does this have to do with us historians and history educators? We have the key to the nation's reading crisis, and we've been ignoring it: When it comes to critical reading, history shines. Hardly anything approaches it in its demands for analysis and thinking.
                                                                Joy Hakim

Teaching with *A History of US* gives you an unparalleled opportunity to focus on literacy. As the author has noted, "Nonfiction is the literary form of our time." Joy Hakim's highly readable nonfiction is a unique tool for teaching strategic reading skills.

READING STRATEGIES AND SKILLS

In order to help your students get the most out of their reading, the Teaching Guides include activities that focus on reading skills as well as reading strategies.

Reading Skills deal with what students actively do with the nonfiction text. The Reading Skills activities in the chapter lesson plans help students identify, evaluate, interpret, understand, and use the following nonfiction elements:

- Text Structure: main idea/supporting details, sequence, comparing and contrasting, question and answer, cause and effect
- Text Features: margin notes, special sections, captions, headings, typeface
- Visual Aids: photographs, paintings, illustrations, political cartoons
- Graphic Aids: graphs, tables, charts, timelines
- Maps: political, physical, historical, special purpose
- Point of View: author's voice and opinion
- Source Material: primary and secondary sources
- Rhetorical Devices: word choice, imagery, connotation/denotation, persuasion, fact and opinion, analogy

Reading Strategies are the intellectual strategies necessary for readers to use their reading skills. Following the ideas of reading authority Janet Allen, these can be categorized as follows:

- Questioning: creating questions to aid with previewing, recalling, and deeper understanding of the text
- Predicting: focusing and guiding reading by previewing text elements and posing questions to be answered
- Visualizing: identifying and using language and imagery to infer, make connections to the text, and predict
- Inferring: identifying text clues and background knowledge to make inferences; using inferences to make predictions and draw conclusions

- **Connecting:** making personal connections to the text, seeing connections between texts, seeing connections between world events and the text
- **Analyzing:** recognizing the relationship between author's intention and author's words, determining author's purpose, understanding how parts of the text work together, using material from the text to support response to the text
- **Synthesizing:** creating an original idea, new line of thinking, or other new creation by combining related ideas

Each Reading Skill activity is related to one of the Reading Strategy categories.

NOTE You probably present material to your students in a variety of ways. There are times you may read aloud to the class or in small groups. Perhaps you'll find it best to have volunteers read aloud—or have the class read silently. You'll find that *A History of US* allows you to vary your approach to suit your schedule and your goals.

LITERACY HANDBOOK: *READING HISTORY*

Reading History is written by Janet Allen, one of American's most prominent literacy advocates. Engaged in the blossoming campaign to integrate literacy and history, Allen provides valuable strategies for teaching nonfiction, taking all examples directly from *A History of US*. Allen says:

> *For the past several years, many content teachers have voiced a common complaint: As we teach and learn with a generation of children who have been raised on technology and sophisticated media, it becomes increasingly difficult to entice them into reading content textbooks.* Reading History *has been written to help you teach your students effective strategies for reading* A History of US *as well as other nonfiction. It is filled with practical ideas for making reading history accessible for even your most reluctant readers.*

ASSESSMENT AND *A HISTORY OF US*

Author Joy Hakim intentionally omits from her books the kinds of section, chapter, and unit questions that are used to review and assess learning in standard textbooks. It is her purpose to engage readers in learning—and loving—history. Rather than interrupt student reading, all assessment instruments for *A History of US* appear in the Teaching Guides.

IN THE TEACHING GUIDES

Ask, Discuss, and Write sections in each chapter lesson plan check students' understanding of chapter content.

Summarizing the Part includes questions for discussion or writing, and activities that help students identify major concepts and themes.

Check-Up pages review content for each Part. These are reproducible pages that appear at the end of each Teaching Guide.

Child labor in mill

Frederick Douglass

HISTORICAL OVERVIEW

Unless a powerful remedy is promptly applied, nothing will prevent them [the Americans] from crossing and penetrating into our provinces on the other side [of the Mississippi].

Baron de Carondelet, the governor of Louisiana, made these remarks in 1794, when he saw the United States poised on the eastern edge of the Mississippi. As Carondelet predicted, the Americans indeed crossed the Mississippi by gaining Louisiana.

By the 1820s the existence of a broad new frontier to settle created powerful bonds of union among Americans. Many Americans thought of progress as a way to achieve such lofty ideals as freedom, equality, and "the pursuit of happiness." Their roving spirit led them into lands not owned by the United States—Texas, Oregon, and California.

In Oregon, the United States avoided war with Great Britain (which also claimed the area) through treaty. Conflicts over lands in Texas and the rest of the Southwest, where people of Spanish ancestry had long-standing ties to the region, went differently.

Fired by the spirit of manifest destiny, some Americans thought it was their right and duty to spread United States culture and government to the Pacific. Mexico, however, which had gained independence from Spain in 1821, saw Americans as foreign lawbreakers.

First, the Texas Revolution erupted, followed by a war between Mexico and the United States over disputed territory in Texas and other lands in the Southwest. Some Americans objected to the war's injustice. But few listened, especially when gold turned up in California with the ink barely dry on the Treaty of Guadalupe Hidalgo. In less than a year, California had enough people to enter the Union.

Admission of new states tested the United States's principles of liberty and equality. When western territories applied for admission to the Union, some Americans wanted to bring them in as slave states. When Northern states balked, a crisis resulted. Hard-won compromises—first the Missouri Compromise of 1820 and then the Compromise of 1850—saved the Union. But peace proved to be short-lived.

By 1850, transportation and communication systems followed the settlers westward, making it possible for one government to rule a continental republic. A spirit of reform expanded education and the rights of women. Writers and artists celebrated the nation. However, the spread of slavery into the western territories threatened American democracy. Two events made compromise all but impossible. First, in 1854, the Kansas-Nebraska Act opened a huge chunk of the West to popular sovereignty. In 1857, the Dred Scott decision took regulation of slavery in the territories out of the hands of Congress.

As the 1850s drew to a close, slaves tried to escape by the thousands along the Underground Railroad. Northerners defied fugitive slave laws, prompting many Southerners to think about leaving the Union. When Abraham Lincoln won the 1860 presidential election on an antislavery platform, the stage was set for civil war.

The story of United States expansion and the march of events that led to the Civil War form the story of Book Five.

TEACHING STRATEGIES FOR BOOK FIVE

Heading Westward

INTRODUCING PART 1

In 1800, the prairies west of the Mississippi still belonged to the Native Americans. Speaking of the years 1800-1820, a Pawnee named Curly Chief remarked: "I heard that long ago there . . . were no people in this country except Indians. After that the people began to hear of men that had white skins; they have been seen far to the east." Part 1 tells about the explorers and pioneers who opened the door to the West.

Preface   Antebellum, *Student Book page 9*
Chapter 1   The Long Way West, *Student Book page 13*
Chapter 2   Mountain Men, *Student Book page 16*
Chapter 3   Riding the Trail to Santa Fe, *Student Book page 21*
Chapter 4   Susan Magoffin's Diary, *Student Book Page 26*
Chapter 5   Pioneers: Taking the Trail West, *Student Book page 30*
Chapter 6   Getting There, *Student Book page 38*
Chapter 7   Latter-Day Saints, *Student Book page 43*

SETTING GOALS

The goals for students in Part 1 are to:
- explain why westward expansion was or was not in the country's national interest.
- describe the life and economy of the mountain men.
- explain the impact of western migration from the Native American's point of view.
- identify the lands affected by western migration.

GETTING INTERESTED

1. Have students turn to the illustration on page 12. Ask: Why do you think the pioneers headed west? *(to find land and riches)* Tell students that between 1790 and 1800 the nation's population had jumped by 35 percent, and it jumped another 36 percent by 1810. Ask: What problems might this create in a still largely agricultural nation? *(There was less farmland to support the population.)*

2. Link the ideas of expansion and conflict by asking students to think what would happen if their school population suddenly tripled. What conflicts might develop? *(People might compete for resources or space.)* Why would conflicts develop between pioneers and Native Americans? *(The pioneers were headed to lands where Native Americans lived.)*

Working with Timelines
Have students construct a timeline on which they record significant dates and events in Part 1. Working individually or as a class, have students begin their timelines in 1803 with the Louisiana Purchase and end in 1849 with the pioneers following the Overland Trail. Students should take notes as they read and make entries on the timeline after completing each chapter.

Using Maps
Have students turn to the map on page 41. Then, to help students appreciate the great distances in the United States, have them use the classroom wall map of the United States and the map scale to calculate the approximate distance pioneers traveled from Independence, Missouri, to San Francisco. Ask: How many days would it take an ox-drawn wagon to go from Independence to San Francisco if it averaged 15 miles a day?

12 | LIBERTY FOR ALL?

TEACHING CHAPTER 1 pages 13-15 1 class period, 35-50 minutes

The Long Way West

In the early 19th century, most Americans looked upon the Great Plains as a desert. They knew little of the land beyond. They thought the land acquired in the Louisiana Purchase (which almost doubled the area of the United States) was uninhabitable. They were happy to leave it to the Native Americans.

ASK

1. How did the Louisiana Purchase change the boundaries of the United States? *(It added a huge amount of land between the Mississippi River and the Rocky Mountains.)*
2. Why did the Spanish, French, English, and Americans feel they could buy and sell Native American lands west of the Mississippi? *(They viewed Native Americans as having no rights; they felt there was room for both Native Americans and settlers.)*
3. What do we now call the land of the Louisiana Purchase? *(Great Plains)* Why did mapmaker Edwin James call this area the Great American Desert? *(The Long expedition thought the land was uninhabitable.)*
4. Have students identify the Louisiana Purchase on Resource 2 (TG page 72).

DISCUSS

1. Have students describe the western boundaries of the country after the Louisiana Purchase. Which countries controlled the land on these boundaries? *(In the Southwest and beyond the Rocky Mountains was California, which was controlled by Spain. In the Northwest was the Oregon Country, to which Britain had a claim.)*
2. In what way was Stephen Long's expedition a success? In what way was it a failure? *(Success: He explored land and made observations. Failure: He didn't understand that the Great Plains could be a good place for farmers.)*
3. **Sourcebook** As students follow along, read aloud Source #31. Using a wall map, have students locate the places that Lewis mentions.

WRITE

Have students write a letter to President Monroe giving two or three reasons why further exploration in the West is unnecessary. Encourage students to support their arguments with a quotation from Stephen Long's letter to Monroe.

Ponder
If you had been exploring the Great Plains with Stephen Long, would you have wanted to live there? What would have swayed your decision?

Question Chart

LITERACY LINKS

Words to Discuss

- iron horse
- bluff
- uninhabitable
- habitation
- inhabitants

Have students use a dictionary to find the two meanings of *bluff*. Then have them look up *inhabitants*, *habitation*, and *uninhabitable*. Ask students to write the definition for each word and then use each word in a sentence. Ask: Why was "iron horse" a good name for railroad trains? *(They were made of iron and were fast, like horses.)*

Reading Skills
Understanding Text Features

Explain that artists and mapmakers often traveled with explorers to draw the land, wildlife, scenery, and people they encountered. Have students read the captions on pages 14 and 15. Ask these questions. VISUALIZING

- When were these pictures made? *(about 1819)*
- How do they help us know what America was like before the west was settled? *(They show the artist's impressions of the Native Americans and what the land looked like.)*

Skills Connection
History/Geography

Have students turn to the map on pages 216-217. Ask: After the original 13 states, what was the next big area of land gained by the United States? *(The lands colored green on the map, which were gained by the Treaty of Paris with Great Britain in 1783.)* How many years later did Thomas Jefferson make the Louisiana Purchase? *(20 years)*

PART 1 | 13

TEACHING CHAPTER 2 pages 16-20   1 class period, 35-50 minutes

Mountain Men

A group of rough-and-tumble fur traders known as mountain men took the lead in blazing trails across Native American lands west of the Mississippi.

ASK

1. Who were the mountain men? *(They were fur trappers and traders who lived like the Indians in the West.)*
2. What was the purpose of the rendezvous that William Ashley arranged? *(It was a yearly get-together where mountain men, fur traders, and Indians got together to trade and socialize.)*
3. How was Jedediah Smith different from other mountain men? *(He didn't drink or smoke; he was religious and thought he could help the nation grow.)* What were his accomplishments as an explorer? *(He re-found South Pass, which was a gap in the Rockies; he was the first white man to go overland from the United States to California.)*

Ponder
Because of overtrapping, beavers almost became extinct. If the mountain men had known that would happen, would they have acted differently?

Question Chart

DISCUSS

1. Why might Jim Bridger's stories of the places he had seen have sounded like tall tales? *(He spoke of a forest where trees had turned to stone and of springs that had hot water.)*
2. What geographic features of the West did the mountain men "discover"? *(South Pass, Beckwourth Pass, petrified forest, Great Salt Lake)*
3. How did the popularity of a clothing style in Paris affect the mountain men in the Rockies 5,000 miles away? *(Trapping and trading beavers was no longer needed when beaver hats went out of fashion; many mountain men then became guides.)*

WRITE

Have students suppose they are mountain men attending a rendezvous. Ask them to write a journal entry using as many of the following terms as they can: *Rocky Mountains, rendezvous, grizzly, mountain man, South Pass, castor, beaver hats.*

LITERACY LINKS

Words to Discuss

rendezvous   trekked
mountain man petrified

Have students list the terms in alphabetical order and use a dictionary to determine the meaning of *trekked* (traveled with difficulty) and *petrified* (changed into stone). Then ask students to construct a sentence that includes all four terms.

Reading Skills
Understanding Graphic Aids

Direct students to the map on page 18 and read its title. Have students locate the Rocky Mountains. Explain that the numbered text at the bottom of the map corresponds to the numbers on the map. As volunteers read each numbered item, have students locate the corresponding number on the map.

After students find numbers 7, 8, and 9 on the map, discuss how the symbols of a lizard, cactus, and arrow help illustrate events. Explain that the map gives further details about Smith's travels as explained in the text. Have students use both the text on page 19 and the information on the map to answer questions such as the following. CONNECTING

- In what region is the South Pass? *(Wyoming)*
- Who helped Smith find the pass? *(Crow Indians)*
- In what mountains is the South Pass located? *(Rockies)*

14 | LIBERTY FOR ALL?

TEACHING CHAPTER 3 pages 11-25 1 class period, 35-50 minutes

Riding the Trail to Santa Fe

As the mountain men were exploring the West, U.S. explorers also found their way into the Southwest, to lands claimed by Mexico. The lure of trade led them to carve out a trail to Santa Fe, paving the way for later United States expansion into New Mexico.

ASK

1. What parts of Zebulon Pike's account of the present-day Southwest interested people the most? *(a towering mountain now known as Pikes Peak and a rich Spanish town called Santa Fe)*
2. Why did most people travel the Santa Fe Trail? *(to get rich, for adventure, to see new lands)*
3. How did the governor of Mexico encourage people to travel to Santa Fe? *(He said that people from the United States were welcome to trade.)*

DISCUSS

1. How did both the explorers and the people in Santa Fe feel about meeting each other? What does Josiah Gregg write about them? *(They were excited and curious; both the wagoneers and the people of Santa Fe dressed up; wagoneers showed off; local people crowded around them.)*
2. There were many different kinds of people in Santa Fe when the wagon trains arrived. Give examples. *(There were Mexicans, Spaniards, Native Americans, Americans, French, Germans, Poles.)*

Ponder
Consider Joy Hakim's question in the margin note on page 24: "When the open land was gone, would conditions become less equal?"

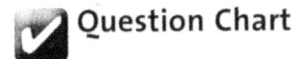 Question Chart

WRITE

Ask students to suppose that it is 1820. They are writing a newspaper column for traders in the 1820s. Have them create a Top Ten list of tips, advising traders on things they need to know for a successful expedition from Missouri to Santa Fe.

LITERACY LINKS

Words to Discuss

pinnacle   **rawhide**

Have students look in a dictionary to determine the meaning of the words. Ask: Did Pike reach the pinnacle of Pikes Peak? *(no)* Ask students to create another tongue-twister using the word *pinnacle*.

Reading Skills
Evaluating Word Choice

Read aloud the Gregg quote on page 25. If necessary, help students translate the Spanish terms: *Americanos* (Americans), *carros* (carts), *entrada de la caravana* (arrival of the caravan), *leperos* (vagrants or petty thieves), *plaza publica* (public square or plaza). Ask. VIZUALIZING

- What effect does Gregg's use of Spanish words have on the reader? *(The Spanish words make the scene more colorful and realistic—because Spanish was spoken in Santa Fe.)*

Skills Connection
Geography

Have student look at the map on page 23. Ask: What three cities were connected by the Santa Fe Trail? *(Franklin, Independence, Santa Fe.)* Have students trace and label the approximate route of the Santa Fe Trail on Resource 3 (TG page 73).

PART 1 | 15

TEACHING CHAPTER 4 pages 26-29 1 class period, 35-50 minutes

Susan Magoffin's Diary

Twenty-five years after William Becknell's first trading trip to Santa Fe, Susan Magoffin was among the "foreign invaders" who traveled the Santa Fe Trail into Spanish-speaking New Mexico. Her brother-in-law James helped in the bloodless United States takeover of the Mexican territory.

ASK

1. What was Susan Magoffin like? *(cheerful, courageous, a good sport, made the best of things)* Why would those qualities be useful to a pioneer? *(Pioneers faced many difficulties and had to work hard.)*

2. What role did James Magoffin play in the U.S. gaining New Mexico as a territory? *(He persuaded the governor of New Mexico—his brother-in-law—not to fight the U.S. Army.)*

3. How did the Great Potato Famine in Ireland, political unrest in Germany, and joblessness in China contribute to U.S. expansion? *(All three events increased immigration to the United States, which expanded the population, increased the number of people who headed to the West, and helped provide the labor the country needed.)*

Ponder
Most of the people who came to America were poor or persecuted. Why were there few rich immigrants?

Question Chart

DISCUSS

1. Reread the margin note on page 26. From Chief Seattle's point of view, how had the arrival of the white pioneers changed the population? *(The pioneers had replaced the Native Americans who used to cover the land.)* Why might Chief Seattle have said that his people were partly to blame? *(Responses will vary; possibly by agreeing to treaties.)*

2. Which group of people added to the nation's diversity after the United States acquired New Mexico? *(Spanish-speaking people who lived north of present-day Mexico.)*

3. Compare and contrast Susan Magoffin's reasons for migrating west with the reason's people from Europe and Asia immigrated to America? *(Both groups were looking for a new life; Magoffin and some immigrants were looking for adventure; although Magoffin was rich, many immigrants were poor or persecuted and hoped for new opportunities.)*

WRITE

Have students suppose they are newspaper writers in Germany or Ireland in 1845. Have them write articles entitled "Let's Go!" encouraging readers to immigrate to America.

LITERACY LINKS

Words to Discuss

poor law
blight
Great Potato Famine
immigrant

Have students use context to determine the meaning of the words. Ask: How are *blight* and *Potato Famine* connected? *(Blight is a disease that destroyed potatoes and caused Ireland's Great Potato Famine.)*

Reading Skills
Evaluating Point of View

Draw students' attention to the margin note on page 26. Ask these questions. QUESTIONING

- What are Chief Seattle's memories of his people? *(His people were many and they were great.)*
- Who are the "paleface brothers" and what is his attitude toward them? *(The white settlers; he doesn't hate them for what they did.)*
- How does he judge his own people? *(They may have been to blame, too.)*

Skills Connection
Math

The trip from Missouri to Santa Fe was 800 miles and took a month. What was the average daily distance traveled? *(about 26-27 miles)* If an airplane traveled 400 miles per hour, how long would it take to fly the same distance today? *(2 hours)*

16 | LIBERTY FOR ALL?

TEACHING CHAPTER 5
pages 30-37 · 1 class period, 35-50 minutes

Pioneers: Taking the Trail West

Dreams of fertile lands sent thousands of pioneers west on the Oregon Trail—a trail marked by graves, animal carcasses, and discarded personal treasures.

ASK

1. Why did the pioneers head west? *(because they wanted a better life for themselves and their children; because they were adventurous or restless; because they wanted to escape a depression in the East)*
2. What hardships did people endure along the Oregon Trail? *(disease, harsh weather, rough traveling, lack of drinking water, and so on)*
3. Why were the pioneers' wagons called "prairie schooners?" *(Schooners are ships—when the wind filled the canvas that covered the wagons they seemed to sail over the land.)* Why did people often leave their supplies behind on the trail? *(to lighten the load)*
4. Have students identify the Oregon Trail on Resource 3 (TG page 73).

DISCUSS

1. Many pioneers had already suffered because of the economic depression of 1837. How do you think this experience might have affected their feelings about going west? *(Possible responses: It probably strengthened their determination to be successful; it was their only chance to make a living.)*
2. Explain that Charles Dickens was a well-known English writer. Ask: What was Dickens's opinion of St. Louis? *(The French part of it was crumbling but quaint; the new buildings built by Americans were much better. St. Louis would not be as beautiful as Cincinnati.)*

WRITE

Ask students to use the text to list the items that were packed in the pioneer's wagons. Then ask students to write a letter postmarked Independence, Missouri, that explains to a relative in the East what they have packed—and why. Students may want to include personal items not mentioned in the text.

Ponder
The people pictured on page 34 were traveling on a trail in Utah in 1867. What do their faces say about the trip?

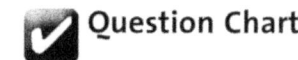 Question Chart

LITERACY LINKS

Words to Discuss

prairie schooner
emigrant
pioneer

Have students define the terms from context. Ask students to find the words *emigrant* and *immigrant* in the dictionary and compare their meanings.

Reading Skills
Evaluating Primary Sources

Help students analyze the primary sources in the chapter. ANALYZING

- What can we learn from Amelia Stewart's diary? *(details of her day and her feelings)*
- What does Jeremiah Fish want to accomplish in his letter? *(convince his friend to move to Iowa)*
- How does Francis Parkman describe Independence? *(crowded, multitude of shops, streets were thronged, incessant hammering)*

Skills Connection
History/Geography

Explain that to reach Fort Boise, Idaho, pioneers on the Oregon Trail crossed many rivers. The wagons traveled across Idaho on the plains south of the Snake River. They forded the Snake at Three Island crossing at Glen's Ferry. That crossing was so difficult that some pioneers avoided it and took a southern bypass that rejoined the trail further north but missed Fort Boise. Students may visit *oregontrailcenter.org* for more information on the Oregon Trail.

PART 1 | 17

TEACHING CHAPTER 6 pages 38-42   1 class period, 35-50 minutes

Getting There

The dangers of travel along the Oregon Trail forged close bonds among pioneers. Following a tradition started by the Pilgrims, many groups wrote compacts to ensure that they carried into the wilderness governments based upon law.

ASK

1. Why did people travel west in wagon trains? *(The trip was too dangerous to attempt alone.)*
2. Why did many people in wagon trains write compacts? *(Since the train was a community, they needed rules to keep order.)*
3. In what place did the Oregon Trail and the California Trail proceed in different directions? *(around South Pass, the pass through the Rockies)* Which mountains did people on the California Trail have to cross? *(Sierra Nevadas)*
4. Have students identify the California Trail on Resource 3 (TG page 73).

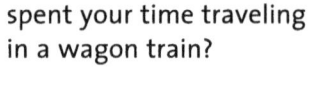

Ponder
How would you have spent your time traveling in a wagon train?

Question Chart

DISCUSS

1. It is about 2,000 miles from Missouri to the West Coast. If you walk 2,000 miles and you average 15 miles a day, how many days will it take you to get there? How many months? *(about 133 days; about 4$^1/_2$ months)*
2. Suppose you had traveled the California Trail to the Humboldt Sink. Would you wish you hadn't come? *(Responses will vary. Some students might question the price of the journey Others may mention the inspiring dreams of a new life.)*

WRITE

Review the Applegate excerpt (pages 38-39) and the Hasting note (page 40). Then ask students to write a list of *Rules to Travel By* that will serve as the bylaws for a wagon train traveling from Independence to Oregon.

LITERACY LINKS

Words to Discuss

wagon train
Humboldt Sink
compact

Ask students to review the meaning of *compact* in the dictionary. Ask: How are *compact* and *wagon train* related? *(People on some wagon trains made a code of laws, or a compact, to govern themselves.)*

Reading Skills
Understanding Rhetorical Devices

Draw students' attention to page 40, where the author asks readers to pretend that they are on the trail to California. Discuss how this technique influences their reading. CONNECTING

- What does the author mention that makes you feel the trip is enjoyable? *(colorful birds, game to eat, children to play with, clear water to drink)*
- How does she make you feel that the trip is difficult? *(mosquitoes, rainstorms, lack of water, rocky mountains, burning sun)*

Meeting Individual Needs
Visual Learners

Have students work in groups to create advertisements for (a) a rendezvous of mountain men along the upper Missouri River, (b) a trade caravan to Santa Fe, or (c) a wagon train to the Oregon Country. Ads should include descriptive pictures.

18 | LIBERTY FOR ALL?

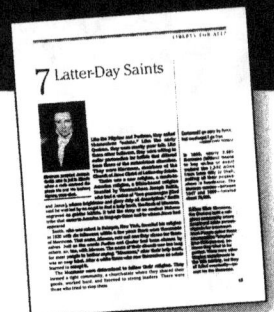

TEACHING CHAPTER 7 pages 43-47   1 class period, 35-50 minutes

Latter-Day Saints

The Mormons were pioneers who had moved again and again in search of religious freedom. Their settlement by the Great Salt Lake of the Utah territory increased the cultural pluralism of our nation.

ASK

1. Who are the Latter-Day Saints? *(a religious group commonly known as Mormons)*
2. What happened at Nauvoo, Illinois, that forced the Mormons to leave? *(People attacked the Mormons, killed Joseph Smith, and destroyed much of the city.)*
3. Why were the Mormons attacked and persecuted? *(Some people may have been jealous of their success; people were angry that the Mormons converted others; some objected to their practice of polygamy.)*
4. Why did Brigham Young lead the Mormons to lands claimed by Mexico? *(He felt leaving the United States was the only way for Mormons to prosper and practice their religion freely; no other pioneers seemed to want the land.)*
5. What did the Mormons achieve in their settlement near Great Salt Lake? *(Mormons built 325 towns, railroads, stores, factories; they farmed and built irrigation projects.)*
6. Have students identify the Mormon Trail from Nauvoo to Salt Lake City on Resource 3 (TG page 73).

Ponder
How did the persecution of the Mormons go against the ideas written in the Constitution?

 **Question Chart**

DISCUSS

1. How did the Mormons help pioneers who were headed west? *(Mormons provided food, horses, and a place to rest.)*
2. Joseph Smith founded the Mormon religion with six followers. Within a few years, there were thousands of Mormons. How do you think that happened? *(Smith must have been a forceful leader, a dynamic speaker; his ideas appealed to people.)*

WRITE

Have students turn to the illustration on page 45. As members of the Mormon community pictured here in Nebraska, they are to write a letter to a friend back in the East describing this part of their journey.

LITERACY LINKS

Words to Discuss

Latter-Day Saints   Mormons
polygamy   pluralism

Have students define or describe the terms from context. Explain that *pluralism* can also be defined as "a form of society in which the members of minority groups maintain their own cultural traditions." Ask students to write a sentence that includes the words *America* and *pluralism*.

Reading Skills
Evaluating Visuals

Have students study the illustrations of the Mormon camp on page 45 and the farm on page 46. INFERRING

- How do these pictures suggest that the Mormons had a strong sense of order? *(They show a very orderly layout of similar buildings.)*
- What do the pictures show about the Mormons' ability to adapt to their environment? *(They used available resources to build; they were successful farmers.)*

Meeting Individual Needs
Auditory Learners

You may want to assist students by scheduling periodic sessions where you or volunteers read the text, emphasizing the main points. Students may take notes, organizing them under section titles such as *Mormon Religion, Persecution, Migration to Utah*, and so on.

PART 1 | 19

SUMMARIZING PART 1

THINKING ABOUT THE THEMES

The following questions will help students relate the book's themes to the content of Part 1. You may wish to use the questions for classroom discussion or have students answer them in written form.

1. Travelers on the Santa Fe Trail, the Oregon Trail, and the Mormon Trail generally had different reasons for heading west. What were they? *(Santa Fe travelers were usually interested in trade. People on the Oregon Trail were interested in settling, starting a new life, and escaping the depression. Mormon travelers were seeking freedom from religious persecution.)*

2. How did the United States expand to include the New Mexico Territory? *(The U.S. claimed the New Mexico Territory after convincing the Spanish governor not to fight.)*

3. Draw students' attention to the other themes that have been posted around the room. Give them the opportunity to explore the relevance of these themes to Part 1. Accept choices that are supported by sound reasoning.

ASSESSING PART 1

Use Check-Up 1 (TG page 64) to assess student learning.

NOTE FROM JOY HAKIM

I want students to read and enjoy all of the chapters in this book. Some chapters need real study, however, while others can be read by students on their own.

PROJECTS AND ACTIVITIES

▶ Monologues from the Trail

Have individuals choose one of the quotations, letters, or diary entries in Part 1 and prepare to deliver the text, or part of the text, as a monologue. Students should practice out loud to try to capture the voice of the author and choose one prop to include in their presentation.

▶ A Western Gazetteer

Have small groups prepare a 15-entry gazetteer for Part 1. Explain that a gazetteer is a geographical dictionary that lists places of interest in alphabetical order and includes brief description of each place. A sample entry might be: *Independence, Missouri: Starting point for travelers on the Santa Fe and Oregon Trails.* Each entry should relate to westward expansion.

▶ Trail Song

Have students write lyrics for a song that pioneers might have sung around the campfire. They may wish to set their lyrics to a song such as "O, Susanna" or another song they're familiar with.

▶ Timeline

Assign groups of students to review and check their individual timelines of the important events described in Part 1. Encourage students to make additions or corrections as necessary.

★★ FACTS TO SHARE ★★

Although the pioneers felt they were facing a wild, new country, Native Americans had the opposite view. Said Chief Luther Standing Bear of the Ogallala Sioux: "We did not think of the great open plains, the beautiful rolling hills, and winding streams with tangled growth, as 'wild.' To us it was tame. Earth was bountiful and we were surrounded with the blessings of the Great Mystery."

20 | LIBERTY FOR ALL?

INTRODUCING PART 2: Extending Boundaries

In 1820, Mexico put General Manuel Mier y Teran in charge of colonization. In 1829, he warned officials in Mexico City that "The North Americans have conquered whatever territory adjoins them" and predicted that the *norteamericanos* would soon grab Mexican lands as well. "There is no physical force that can stop the[ir] entrance," he said. Part 2 traces the flood of settlers that swept Mexico from the Southwest.

Chapter 8   Coast-to-Coast Destiny, *Student Book page 48*
Chapter 9   A Hero of His Times, *Student Book page 54*
Chapter 10 Texas: Tempting and Beautiful, *Student Book page 58*
Chapter 11 Fighting Over a Border, *Student Book page 64*
Chapter 12 There's Gold in Them Hills, *Student Book page 69*

SETTING GOALS

The goals for students in Part 2 are to:
- understand the significance of manifest destiny.
- describe John Frémont's role in the U.S. acquisition of California.
- list the key events leading to Texas independence in 1836.
- analyze the justness of the Mexican War.
- understand the highlights of the California gold rush.

GETTING INTERESTED

1. Write the title of Chapter 8, "Coast-to-Coast Destiny," on the chalkboard. How would you describe the geography of America in terms of "coast"? *(It goes from the Atlantic Coast to the Pacific Coast.)* What does *destiny* mean? *(something that is fated; sure to happen)* Tell students that the title of this Part is "Extending Boundaries." Ask what they think the Part will be about? (*the expansion of the United States from coast to coast*)

2. Which country ceded New Mexico to the United States? *(Mexico)* Have students turn to the Atlas on pages 216 and 217. What other parts of the present-day United States did Mexico control at this time? *(California, Nevada, Utah, part of Colorado)* Have students imagine a U.S. that did not include these states. How would that affect the nation?

Working with Timelines

Most of the events in this Part occur in the 1830s and 1840s. Have students skim the chapters, looking for indications of the conflicts that occur during this time (for instance, conflict over the expansion of U.S. borders). Ask students to begin a timeline for Part 2 in which they note major events, conflicts, and acquisitions that resulted from these conflicts.

Using Maps

The total area of Texas, New Mexico, Arizona, Utah, Nevada, and California is approximately 863,000 square miles, or almost half the size of the U.S. after the Louisiana Purchase. Refer students to the Atlas on pages 216-217 and remind students that the Louisiana Purchase almost doubled the area of the United States. Have students estimate the total number of square miles in the U.S. before and after the Louisiana Purchase and after 1845.

PART 2 | 21

TEACHING CHAPTER 8
pages 48-53 · 1 class period, 35-50 minutes

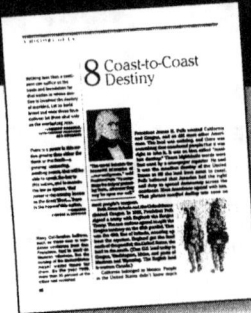

Coast-to-Coast Destiny

The idea of manifest destiny was fueled by the writings of California traveler Richard Henry Dana; the term was first used by John L. O'Sullivan in an influential newspaper editorial in 1845. President James Polk began setting the stage to acquire this land from the Mexicans.

ASK

1. What was manifest destiny? *(the idea that the United States had a right and duty to spread democracy across the continent)*
2. Which countries had claims to lands in the West? *(The British had claims to Oregon and Mexico had claims to California.)*
3. What was the purpose of the Spanish missions? *(to reinforce Spanish claims to California, to grow crops, to teach Christianity to the Indians)* What became of the missions after Mexico won independence from Spain in 1821? *(Mexican Californians took over the missions and turned them into valuable cattle ranches; the Indians did all the hard work.)*
4. How did President Polk want to acquire California? *(buy it)* What was Mexico's response? *(The Mexican government was insulted and said they would not sell it.)*
5. Have students identify the Oregon Country on Resource 2 (TG page 72).

Ponder In 1821, Mexico controlled California. How do you think the Mexicans felt when thousands of Americans from the East began to arrive?

Question Chart

DISCUSS

1. How did Dana's book, O'Sullivan's article, and Leutze's painting contribute to the idea of manifest destiny? *(Dana's book created excitement about California, its land, and its silver, and called for enterprising people to settle there. O'Sullivan's article persuaded people that extending U.S. boundaries to California was inevitable. Leutze's painting showed an almost biblical scene of pioneers going west.)*
2. **Sourcebook** Read aloud excerpts from Source #40 as students follow along. Note especially the definition of *manifest destiny* in the margin note.

WRITE

Have students suppose they are Native Americans living on a ranch in California in 1821. Have them write a journal entry describing a typical day.

LITERACY LINKS

Words to Discuss

49th parallel
manifest destiny
ranchero

Ask: What is the 49th parallel? *(a line of latitude)* Why is it important to the history and geography of the U.S.? *(It marks the northern boundary of the U.S. and was established by a treaty between the U.S. and Britain.)* Where would you find a *ranchero*? *(running a ranch in California)*

Reading Skills
Interpreting Graphics

Have students examine the diagram of the Spanish mission on page 50. INFERRING

- What are some of the activities at the mission? *(weaving, carpentry, gardening)*
- How can you tell the importance of religion? *(The church is the largest building on the premises.)*
- What is the role of the Native Americans? *(They do the hard work.)*

Skills Connection
Art/History

Have students examine the picture *America's Progress* on page 49, painted in 1872 by John Gast. Explain that prints of this painting were very popular and were even included in tourist guides. Point out that the woman in the painting represents *manifest destiny*—a positive, maternal force advancing westward. Ask students to focus on specific details that illustrate the artists' vision of America in 1872. *(telegraph wire, fleeing buffalo and Native Americans, advancing plow and train)*

22 | LIBERTY FOR ALL?

TEACHING CHAPTER 9 pages 54-57   1 class period, 35-50 minutes

A Hero of His Times

John Frémont did more than almost anyone else to secure California for Americans. This controversial man first created interest in the territory and then helped America acquire it from Mexico.

ASK

1. What were John Frémont's accomplishments as an explorer? *(He found and named the Great Basin, understood there was no water route to the Pacific Ocean, and mapped large areas of the West.)*
2. How did Frémont's writings about California influence Americans? *(Frémont was a dramatic writer; his descriptions of California and of his adventures helped convince President Polk and others that America should have California.)*
3. What was the Bear Flag Republic? What happened to it? *(It was an independent California nation established by Americans. It was taken over by the U.S.)*
4. How did the United States acquire California? *(The U.S. declared war on Mexico and claimed it.)*

Ponder
Was Frémont truly a "hero of his time"? Who would be a hero of your time? Why?

 **Question Chart**

DISCUSS

1. What happened to Frémont as a result of his opposition to slavery? *(Frémont lost the presidential election of 1856 at least partly because he was against slavery; during the Civil War, he was fired from the army after giving an order to free slaves in Missouri.)*
2. Explain that some people say that great moments in history are determined by great men or women. Ask: Do you think the United States would have acquired California from Mexico without John Frémont? *(Possible response: The United States probably would have acquired California at some time, but Frémont speeded up the process.)*

WRITE

Have students write an advertisement for John Frémont's book about his expeditions. Include facts about Frémont that would interest readers in the author's life. Adjectives and figurative language will help persuade readers to buy the book.

LITERACY LINKS

Words to Discuss

latitude	topographical
longitude	Great Basin

Ask students to determine the terms' meanings by consulting a dictionary or an atlas. Then have students look at the map on page 55. Ask: Why is this a topographical map? *(It shows details of land features.)* Does the map show lines of latitude or longitude? *(no)*

Reading Skills
Identifying Fact and Opinion
Discuss that opinions cannot be proven, whereas facts can be backed up by evidence. Have students read the margin note on page 54. Have them analyze whether statements are facts or opinions. ANALYZING

- Frémont's background made him restless. *(opinion)*
- Frémont's father was named Charles Fremon. *(fact)*
- (from Pisani's quote on page 57) Frémont's face was full of intelligence. *(opinion)*

Skills Connection
Geography
Explain that the Great Basin has an almost circular shape, bounded by the Rockies to the east and the Sierra Nevada to the west. Then have them locate the Great Basin—the land from northern Nevada to southwestern Oregon—on the climate map in the Atlas on page 220. Direct students to the color key to find the climate of the area. *(dry, temperature varies with latitude)*

TEACHING CHAPTER 10 pages 58-63 1 class period, 35-50 minutes

Texas: Tempting and Beautiful

First the Spanish took what is now Texas from the Indians. Then *anglos* and *tejanos* (Mexican Texans) took it from Mexico. For nearly a decade, Texas existed as an independent republic.

ASK

1. What led to conflict in Texas between Mexicans and settlers from the United States? *(They clashed over religion, slavery, and ideas of self-government and citizenship.)*
2. What happened at the Alamo? *(Two hundred Texans tried to defend the mission against Santa Anna's army. After a twelve-day siege, the Mexicans took the fort, killing all but six defenders. The heroic defense became a rallying point for the Texans.)*
3. How did Sam Houston help Texas gain independence? *(He led the fight at San Jacinto, defeated the Mexicans, and made Santa Anna sign a treaty making Texas independent.)*
4. How would it have affected Congress if Texas were admitted to the union as a slave state? *(The South would have more votes in Congress than the North.)*
5. Have students identify Texas on Resource 2 (TG page 72).

Ponder
What sort of person does his experience as Texas governor in 1861 show Houston to be?

 **Question Chart**

DISCUSS

1. Why did the independence of Texas turn into a conflict in the United States? *(The U.S. gained Texas, but there was conflict over admitting it as a slave state.)*
2. Direct students to the map on page 216 and note that Houston is located near San Jacinto. Then have students use the classroom wall map to compare the size of the Republic of Texas with the present state of Texas. Ask: Which is larger, the republic or the state? *(the state)* From whom will the U.S. acquire the "disputed area?" *(Mexico)*

WRITE

Have students suppose they are soldiers about to join Sam Houston in his pursuit of Santa Anna. They are to write a speech, entitled "Remember the Alamo," in which they try to persuade others to come along.

LITERACY LINKS

Words to Discuss

anglo   tejano
secede abolitionist
secession

Ask: Which two words describe withdrawing from a nation? *(secede, secession)* Which word names a person who is against slavery? *(abolitionist)* What is the difference between an *anglo* and a *tejano*? *(Anglos are English-speaking Americans; tejanos are Spanish-speaking Mexican Texans.)*

Reading Skills
Using Text Organization

Point out that this chapter covers a lot of time—from the 16th century to 1846. Discuss how the author organizes the information. *(chronologically)* Ask: How does this help you understand how Texas became independent? *(The author reviews early Texas history, and then uses time order to give details about the events leading up to independence.)* Have students construct a timeline for 1821-1836 showing the events leading to Texas independence. SYNTHESIZING

Skills Connection
Culture/Language

Many Spanish words have entered American English. Ask the class to take a few minutes to brainstorm common Spanish words and place names in English. Ask volunteers to list on the board students' suggestions, such as *rodeo, macho, taco, arroyo, mesa, adios, Los Angeles, San Francisco, Colorado, Montana*. Then ask them to list the Spanish words the author has included in this chapter. *(presidio, hacienda, vaquero, siesta, tejano, anglo)*

24 | LIBERTY FOR ALL?

TEACHING CHAPTER 11
pages 64-68 · 1 class period, 35-50 minutes

Fighting Over a Border

Conflicts in Texas convinced hotheads on both sides of the Rio Grande that it was time to fight. In the United States, the desire for land proved stronger than the desire for peace. The result was war with Mexico.

ASK

1. The Mexican War was fought over which border? *(the southern border of Texas)* What natural landmark defined the border? *(the Rio Grande)*
2. Besides fighting over the border, why did Americans want to fight the war? *(to bring the American way of life to Mexico, to extend slavery)*
3. How did most Americans feel about the war? *(They were in favor of it.)* Who were some famous people who were against the war? *(Abraham Lincoln, Henry Clay, Frederick Douglas, Walt Whitman)*
4. Have students identify California on Resource 2 (TG page 72).

DISCUSS

1. Read aloud the quotation from Henry Clay on page 65. Ask: How might President Polk have responded to Clay? *(Responses will vary. Polk would have expressed his belief in manifest destiny and replied that Mexicans had started the war by killing Americans.)*
2. How did General Winfield Scott and Zachary Taylor become American heroes? *(They fought and won the Mexican War.)*
3. How did the Treaty of Guadalupe Hidalgo expand U.S. territory? *(It added Texas and California, and stretched the nation's southwestern border to the Pacific Ocean.)*

WRITE

Direct students to the song on page 67. Then ask them to write the lyrics to another song that might have been sung at this time. The song may praise Zachary Taylor and/or Winfield Scott, or it may protest their actions. Students may set their songs to music that's familiar to them.

Ponder
Many people who opposed U.S. actions in the Mexican War spoke out. What guarantees them the right to do so?

Question Chart

LITERACY LINKS

Words to Discuss
war hawk   patriot
aggression

What is a war hawk? *(a person who is in favor of war)* Can a patriot be against a war? Why? *(A patriot is a person who is loyal to his or her country. A patriot can be against a war that he or she thinks is wrong, or is not in the best interest of the country.)* What is aggression? *(an unprovoked attack)*

Reading Skills
Interpreting a Political Cartoon

Turn to the political cartoon on page 66. Help students interpret its meaning. INFERRING

- What did the cartoonist think of Zachary Taylor?
- How does he illustrate his feelings about Taylor?
- If the cartoonist were to express the drawing in words, what might he say? *(Zachary Taylor is responsible for the deaths of many people.)*

Skills Connection
Geography/Math

Draw students' attention to the map on page 66 and to the map key and scale. Have them use a ruler to determine the following distances:

- About how many miles are represented by 1 3/4" on the map? *(600 miles)* by 1/4"? *(about 86 miles)*
- About how far did U.S. troops travel from New Orleans to Mexico City? *(about 1,116 miles)*

Have students pose other questions they can answer by using the distance scale.

PART 2 | 25

TEACHING CHAPTER 12
pages 69-77 — 1 class period, 35-50 minutes

There's Gold in Them Hills

The ink had barely dried on the Treaty of Guadalupe Hidalgo when a single word blazed across the headlines: *Gold!* The word proved a magnet as people from around the world scrambled into California to search for gold.

ASK

1. Why were the prospectors who headed to California called the "forty-niners?" *(because gold fever hit in 1849, the year after gold was found at Sutter's mill)*
2. From the East, what was the longest but easiest route to California? *(by ship around Cape Horn)* the fastest route? *(by boat to Panama, then overland, then by boat up the Pacific coast)* the cheapest route? *(overland across the continental United States)*
3. What people got rich in California during the gold rush? *(storekeepers)* How did they benefit from the law of supply and demand? *(They sold things that everyone needed. Since there were fewer supplies than there were miners, the storekeepers could charge higher prices for the supplies.)*

Ponder
If you were a forty-niner from the East, which route would you have taken to California? Why?

 **Question Chart**

DISCUSS

1. Read aloud the feature on pages 72-73. Ask: How did the Chinese contribute to the U.S. economy and culture? *(They mined gold; merchants imported Chinese goods; opera companies performed.)*
2. When did Americans begin to blame the Chinese for their troubles? *(After people did not find gold, they wanted someone to blame.)* How were the gold bust and nativism connected? *(Help students understand the link between hard times and scapegoating.)*
3. How did the gold rush increase the diversity of the United States? *(People came from China, Japan, and Peru; more Europeans immigrated to the West.)*
4. Have students complete Resource 4 (TG page 74) about the gold rush.

WRITE

Have students suppose they are prospectors in the 1850s. Have them write a letter to a friend about life out West: the work, living quarters, cost of supplies, and town life.

LITERACY LINKS

Words to Discuss

prospector   forty-niner
Know-Nothings   nativism

Ask students which pairs of words are linked, and how. *(The Know-Nothings was the name given to the political party of people who believed in nativism: the belief that only white Anglo-Saxon Protestants were real Americans. Forty-niners were prospectors who looked for gold.)*

Reading Skills
Making Comparisons

Have students create a two-column comparison chart and label the columns *Miners' Lives* and *Merchants' Lives*. Have them complete the chart with details from the text in these categories: difficulty of work, rewards from work, nationalities of workers, cost of living. After students complete their charts, ask: What other categories of information would be interesting to compare the lives of merchants and miners? *(Responses will vary.)* QUESTIONING

Skills Connection
Science/Technology

Have students use an encyclopedia to find out more about gold. Have them find the answers to these questions:
- Why is gold so precious?
- What are its most common uses?
- What are the different kinds of gold?
- Where are the largest deposits of gold in the world today?

26 | LIBERTY FOR ALL?

SUMMARIZING PART

THINKING ABOUT THE THEMES

The following questions will help students relate the book's themes to the content of Part 2. You may wish to use the questions for classroom discussion or have students answer them in written form.

1. How did the United States expand its territory after the Louisiana Purchase? *(It gained vast lands in the West, including the Oregon Country, Texas, and California.)*
2. How did the expansion of the United States lead to conflicts with Mexico? *(Both Texas and California had belonged to Mexico; the U.S. fought in Texas to gain that land, and fought the Mexican War to gain California.)*
3. How was the idea of manifest destiny not good for Mexicans, Native Americans, Africans, and Chinese? *(Manifest destiny led to the enslavement of Africans in Texas, the taking of land belonging to Mexicans and Native Americans, and the denial of human rights for Chinese immigrants.)*
4. Draw students' attention to the other themes that have been posted around the room. Give them the opportunity to explore the relevance of these themes to Part 2. Accept choices that are supported by sound reasoning.

ASSESSING PART 2

Use Check-Up 2 (TG page 65) to assess student learning.

NOTE FROM JOY HAKIM

Between 1849 and 1863, gold miners put more than $200 million in gold into circulation in the United States. That caused inflation in the 1850s, which gives you an opportunity to talk about economic cycles. The more money there is, the less it is worth. In inflationary times, people spend more, which stimulates the economy. But their savings are worth less—and that leads to trouble.

PROJECTS AND ACTIVITIES

▶ Texas Heroes

Have students create a book entitled *Texas Heroes* to tell the story about the fight for Texas independence. Have small groups use Resource 5 (TG page 75) to write a biographical sketch, with an illustration, of significant figures in the struggle. Students may use the encyclopedia or the Internet to learn more information. Then have groups compile their biographies into one volume.

▶ Gettin' Old Lookin' for Gold

Ask students to write a poem or a limerick that expresses the hard times of a gold miner. Then hold a reading where students present their work to the class.

▶ Timeline

Have students expand the timeline that they constructed in Chapter 10 that showed events leading to Texas independence. Ask them to continue the timeline to show the events through 1848 that led to the establishment of Texas's southern border.

▶ Political Cartoon

Have students create a political cartoon reflecting their ideas about the Mexican War or gold fever in California. Students may wish to work in pairs: one to draw the cartoon, the other to write the caption.

★★ FACTS TO SHARE ★★

At the start of the gold rush, in 1849, the California Trail witnessed America's first traffic jams. For every one person on the trail in 1848 there were 50 in 1849, and six-mile-long wagon trains inched along the trail. A Mormon named John D. Lee noted the endless dust created by the wagons, the smell of dead animals, and the piles of litter including stoves, clothes, wagons, and tools. By 1855, 100,000 travelers had used the California Trail.

Reaching Across Land and Sea

As the United States began to tie the continent together with transportation and communication networks, clipper ships connected the nation to ports around the globe. an 1852 newspaper editorial noted: "It seems we are to send a fleet to Japan. The interes of American trade require that commercial communication be opened with that . . . region." Part 3 tells about the United States' march across land and sea.

Chapter 13 Clipper Ships and Pony Express, *Student Book page 78*
Chapter 14 Flying by Stagecoach, *Student Book page 83*
Chapter 15 Arithmetic by Sea, *Student Book page 85*
Chapter 16 Thar She Blows! *Student Book page 90*
Chapter 17 A Boy from Japan, *Student Book page 95*

SETTING GOALS

The goals for students in Part 3 are to:
- predict the results of the invention of the telegraph.
- explain the experience of stagecoach rides and clipper ships.
- retell Nakahama Manjiro's travels to America.

GETTING INTERESTED

1. Ask students to use the classroom wall map to name a North American city that is at least 2,000 miles from your community. Ask: What are the different ways you can get message to that city, and how long does it take? *(Mail, telephone, e-mail, cell phone, travel; all can be within one day.)*
2. Have students skim through Chapters 13-17, looking at the pictures. Ask: What were some of the "speedy and easy communications" that linked East and West in the mid-1800s? *(Pony Express, clipper ships, telegraph, Morse Code)*

Working with Timelines
Direct students to the Chronology of Events on page 199. Have them read the entries for 1830, 1844, 1850, and 1860. Ask: What kinds of events occurred on these dates? *(Events that concern transportation, communication, or commerce.)* Have students begin a timeline on which to record significant events in Part 3, taking notes as they read and making entries after each appropriate chapter. Remind them to include the dates and events mentioned above.

Using Maps
Refer students to the maps on pag 81 and 98. Ask: In what ways do these maps show how Americans were involved in expanding trade, commerce, and communication? *(The Pony Express connected California with Missouri; whalir ships traveled the seas.)* Help students understand that in the mid-1800s, the United States had begun to link the Atlantic and the Pacific coasts, while at th same time establishing global networks c trade.

28 | LIBERTY FOR ALL?

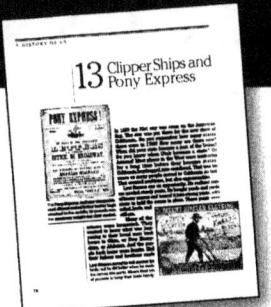

TEACHING CHAPTER 13   pages 78-84   1 class period, 35-50 minutes

Clipper Ships and Pony Express

The billowing sails of clipper ships and the pounding hooves of the Pony Express captured the fast pace of growth in the mid-1800s.

ASK

1. What is the furthest distance you could send a letter by Pony Express? *(from St. Joseph, Missouri, to Sacramento, California)* How long would it take for the letter to arrive? *(10 days)*
2. Why was *Flying Cloud* a good name for a clipper ship that sailed around Cape Horn? *(Clipper ships were the fastest ships in the world. They made the Boston-Cape Horn-San Francisco trip in about three months, as opposed to the 8-9 months of regular ships.)*
3. What is Morse Code? *(A code matching short and long electrical pulses to letters. The pulses could be sent along a wire in dots and dashes, which could then be translated into words by the receiver.)*
4. How did Morse's telegraph gain acceptance *(The telegraph message from Baltimore to Washington announcing Henry Clay's nomination for president made people see the value of the telegraph.)* How did the invention of the telegraph affect the Pony Express? *(The Pony Express went out of business.)*

Ponder
What qualities would a successful Pony Express rider need to have?

 Question Chart

DISCUSS

1. Why did westward expansion create a demand for the development of transportation and communication? *(People wanted to stay in touch with each other through letters, trade, and travel.)*
2. What were the advances in transportation and communication that westward expansion brought about? *(private postal services, Pony Express, stagecoaches, clipper ships, telegraph)*

WRITE

Draw students' attention to the ad for Pony Express riders quoted in the margin note on page 79. Have them reply to the ad, indicating interest in the job.

LITERACY LINKS

Words to Discuss

Levis
clipper ship
telegraph
Pony Express
elevation

After discussing the other words, ask students to use the dictionary to define *elevation* as it refers to the earth's surface. *(height above the earth's surface or sea level)* Ask: How do you think the elevator got its name? *(It is a machine that lifts things and people up.)*

Reading Skills
Analyzing Word Choice

Direct students to the last paragraph on page 81. Ask these questions.
CONNECTING

- What does the author mean by "an idea volcano had erupted in the United States"? *(There was an outpouring of inventions and useful ideas.)*
- What "idea volcano" has occurred in recent times? *(electronics, computers, communications)*

Skills Connection
Reading an Elevation Map

Direct students to the elevation map on page 81. Reinforce the meaning of *elevation*. Point out that the graph above the map gives the elevation of certain places on the map. Ask:
- What is the elevation of Salt Lake City? *(5,000 feet)*
- What was the highest point on the Pony Express route? *(South Pass)* What is its elevation? *(8,000 feet)*
- What was the lowest point? *(Sacramento)*

PART 3 | 29

TEACHING CHAPTER 14   pages 85-89   1 class period, 35-50 minutes

Flying by Stagecoach

Rumbling from Missouri to California, the stagecoach became a symbol of the Old West. For a time, it was the fastest way to get from Missouri to California.

ASK

1. How would you describe a stagecoach? *(a low coach with seats inside and on top of it, pulled by a team of horses)* What did a stagecoach carry? *(mail and passengers)*
2. What native animal could be seen from the early stagecoaches? *(buffalo)*
3. How were Rebecca Yokum's experiences with Native Americans different from experiences other people had? *(She saw Indians dancing around campfires; Indians had killed the station agents and passengers on another coach.)*
4. Have students complete Resource 6 (TG page 76) to learn more about stagecoaches.

Ponder
It took Rebecca Yokum 21 days to get to California. If you had 21 days to travel, where would you go?

Question Chart

DISCUSS

1. What hardships does Yokum mention in her account of stagecoach travel? *(not being able to change clothes; sleeping sitting up, mother holding infant in her lap, lost luggage; only 10 minutes at rest stops; bumpy ride; fear of Indian attacks)* From Rebecca's account, what other hardships do you think traveler's experienced? *(little time to prepare and eat food, poor bathroom facilities, few provisions for illness, cramped quarters, dusty or dirty ride)*
2. Direct students to the feature on pages 86-88. Ask: Who do you think were important presidents? Why? *(Responses will vary.)* Which of these presidents added territory to the U.S. during their administrations? *(Jefferson, Polk, Tyler)*

WRITE

Have students suppose that Rebecca Yokum is a friend. It is 1860 and she has invited them to travel to California with her in the stagecoach. Students are to write a letter, telling her why they will or will not join her.

LITERACY LINKS

Words to Discuss

stagecoach

Stagecoach is a compound word: it is made up of two words. Ask: How does the word *stagecoach* describe a form of transportation? *(A stagecoach is a coach that travels in stages. It stops after a certain period of time to change horses and then travels the next stage of the journey.)*

Reading Skills
Evaluating Primary and Secondary Sources

Elicit that both the author and Rebecca tell the story of Rebecca's journey. Ask these questions.
ANALYZING

- How do we know which are Rebecca's words? *(italics)*
- Why might the author choose to tell the story this way? *(Rebecca's words give a firsthand account; by addng her own words, the author presents information not included in Rebecca's account.)*

Meeting Individual Needs
Auditory Learners

Read aloud Rebecca's words as students follow along in the text. Direct them to each page as you read and have them look for the text in italics. Ask: Do the excerpts tell us about one day in Rebecca's journey or different days?

30 | LIBERTY FOR ALL?

TEACHING CHAPTER 15
pages 90-94 — 1 class period, 35-50 minutes

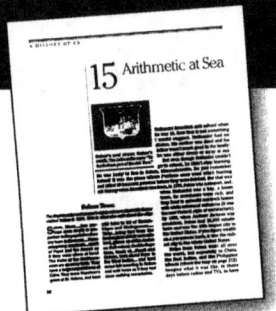

Arithmetic at Sea

Britain might still rule the seas, but in the mid-1800s the United States was fast developing the technology and skills to navigate the world's ocean routes. Leading the way were New England merchant-mariners such as Nathaniel Bowditch.

ASK

1. Why was Salem, Massachusetts, such a rich city? *(It was a seaport whose people had become rich because of ocean trade.)* What items did the Salem sailors bring back home? Where did these items come from? *(spices, teas, rugs, toys, dried figs, and silk; China, East Indies, West Indies, Philippine Islands, Azores, South America, Mediterranean)*
2. On what did Nathaniel Bowditch base his system for finding latitude and longitude? *(on mathematical calculations based on location of the stars)* Why was his book *The New American Practical Navigator* a best-seller? *(It explained his system of navigation and was bought by sailors all over the world.*

DISCUSS

1. Why was it remarkable that young Nathaniel Bowditch grew up to became the author of *The New American Practical Navigator*? *(He had left school as a boy and studied mathematics and other subjects on his own in libraries.)*
2. What do you think would have been exciting about living in Salem? *(Responses will vary. It was a bustling place whose sailors had tales from faraway places; foreign goods were available; people could learn to become sailors or navigators; there was a big library; the buildings were splendid and new.)*

Ponder
Although there were many dangers to sea travel in the 1700s, most Salem boys wanted to become sailors. Why do you suppose they were tempted?

 **Question Chart**

WRITE

Ask students to imagine what it might have been like to go to sea at age 13—as Yankee boys sometimes did. Have students write a letter home to Salem from such a boy. Ask them to give the date and the name of the place they are writing from.

LITERACY LINKS

Words to Discuss

rigging   latitude
navigator longitude

After students determine the meaning of *rigging*, ask them to write one or two sentences in which they include all of the vocabulary words.

Reading Skills
Evaluating Visuals

Ask students to preview the chapter by looking at the diagrams and illustrations. ANALYZING

- What do you think this chapter will be about? *(navigation, boat-building, seamen)*
- What can you tell about the man in the portrait on page 91? *(From all the books and the bust on the left, we can tell that he draws knowledge from the past; his glasses tell us he's been reading; the papers tell us he's probably been writing.)*

Skills Connection
Language/History

Tell students that many idioms, or phrases, in modern English come from our seafaring past. *Knowing the ropes* (page 92) is one example. Share with students other expressions with nautical roots such as *doldrums* (depression, from a windless area near Bermuda); *come aboard* (join in); and *swallow it hook, line and sinker* (being gullible, accepting without questioning).

PART 3 | 31

TEACHING CHAPTER 16 pages 95-101   1 class period, 35-50 minutes

Thar She Blows!

For New Englanders, whales provided much of the lifeblood of commerce. Nobody knew in the mid-1800s that these gigantic mammals would someday face the threat of extinction.

ASK

1. Who inspired the Puritans to begin whaling? *(the Indians on Nantucket Island who went out in boats and harpooned whales near the shore)*
2. What parts of the whale were used? What were they used for? *(blubber—oil for lamps; spermaceti—candles; ambergris—perfume; whalebone—corsets and buggy whips; ivory teeth—decorative items that were often carved in scrimshaw)*
3. Where were the best whaling grounds? *(Pacific Ocean)*
4. What was "trying"? *(the process of converting whale blubber to clean, clear, whale oil by boiling it in a huge cauldron)*

Ponder
In the 1800s, being a whaler was considered by many to be the world's riskiest profession. What might be the riskiest profession today?

Question Chart

DISCUSS

1. What do you think was the most dangerous part of whaling? *(Responses will vary; being killed by whales, slipping overboard to the sharks, fires from the trying process, sinking of ship or whaling boat)*
2. What about a whale makes it possible for them to be captured? *(Whales must come to the surface to breathe air; when they did so, the whalers could harpoon them.)*
3. Who might you meet aboard a whaling ship? *(women, children, officers descended from the British, Native Americans, Portuguese, blacks, Pacific Islanders)* What might this suggest about New Englanders' attitudes about people? *(It suggests that they accepted a diversity of people.)*

WRITE

Have students work in pairs to write a poem about whaling. They can use the title of the chapter as the title of the poem. They may be inspired by the vivid language the author uses to capture the adventure of whaling and the magnificence of whales. Their poems do not have to rhyme.

LITERACY LINKS

Words to Discuss

Nantucket sleigh ride
mate
ambergris

Which two words describe the crew or the crew's activities aboard a whaling boat? *(Nantucket sleigh ride, mate)* Ask: What would your version of a "Nantucket sleigh ride" be? What is ambergris? *(a bacterial substance found in some whales that is used by perfume makers)*

Reading Skills
Evaluating Word Choice

Point out that the author conveys the excitement of whaling by using comparisons *(whale and school bus)*, metaphors *(goliaths of the ocean)*, and strong adjectives *(towering waterspout)*. Have partners reread the chapter and list vivid words and phrases Joy Hakim uses to describe whales and whaling. When they are finished, you can use these lists to illustrate how authors use figurative language to help readers visualize events. VIZUALIZING

Skills Connection
Conservation/Ecology

Discuss the 1985 ban on commercial whaling that the author mentions on page 100. Discuss how economics can affect the environment. (Remind students how the beaver population fell because of European fur trappers.) Discuss how whale-watching expeditions and African photographic safaris can both help economic activity and promote animal conservation.

32 | LIBERTY FOR ALL?

TEACHING CHAPTER 17 pages 102-106   1 class period, 35-50 minutes

A Japanese Boy in America

John Manjiro gave the United States one of the first inside looks at feudal Japan. A few decades later, he watched as Matthew Perry pried his way into Edo, the capital of Japan.

ASK

1. What are the characteristics of a feudal society? *(people are divided into social classes, limited ownership of land, no opportunity to move from one class to another)*
2. After he rescued Manjiro and the other boys, why couldn't Captain Whitfield take them back to Japan? *(Japan was closed to foreigners.)*
3. What was the purpose of Matthew Perry's naval expedition to Japan? *(to open Japan to trade)* What were some of its effects on Japan? *(expanded commerce, introduced new technology, ended isolation)*

Ponder
Why did the emperor of Japan change his mind about trading with the United States?

Question Chart

DISCUSS

1. How were Manjiro and Bowditch similar? *(Manjiro and Bowditch were both determined students; they advanced navigation techniques for their countries; Manjiro translated Bowditch's book into Japanese.)*
2. What role did Manjiro play in opening trade between the U.S. and Japan? *(He spoke to Japan's shogun about the United States. He may have influenced the shogun to agree to trade.)*

WRITE

Ask students to suppose they are Nakahama Manjiro, who has arrived in the United States. They are to write a letter to a friend back home, describing how different life is here from life in Japan.

LITERACY LINKS

Words to Discuss

- shogun
- Samurai
- daimyo
- feudal system
- serf
- peasants

After students use context and a dictionary to determine the meaning of each word, ask them to make a labeled diagram showing the social structure of feudal Japan. Have students include the English equivalents of the words in parentheses *(shogun—military governor; daimyo—lords; samurai—knights)*.

Reading Skills
Comparing and Contrasting

Help students understand the comparisons the author makes to portray feudal Japan. INFERRING

- To whom is the Japanese peasant class compared? *(Russian serfs)*
- How were Russian serfdom and American slavery different? *(Slave children could be sold in America; children of serfs in Russia were not sold.)*
- How did America compare to Japan for Manjiro? *(more freedom)*

Skills Connection
Geography

Explain to students that the Suez Canal across Egypt opened in 1869 and the Panama Canal opened in 1914. Have them use the world map on pages 214-215 to determine what routes ships from New England might have taken to Japan after Perry's visit in 1853. What route might ships take after the Panama Canal opened?

PART 3 | 33

SUMMARIZING PART

THINKING ABOUT THE THEMES

The following questions will help students relate the book's themes to the content of Part 3. You may wish to use these questions for classroom discussion or have students answer them in written form.

1. What advances in communication and transportation occurred as a result of the coast-to-coast expansion of the United States? *(The Pony Express and the telegraph allowed people to communicate over long distances. Stagecoaches made travel faster. Better ships and navigation techniques allowed speedy travel by ship.)*

2. How was international trade expanded in the 1800s? *(Whalers traded all over the world; Japan opened its doors to trade.)*

3. Draw students' attention to the other themes that have been posted around the room. Give them the opportunity to explore the relevance of these themes to Part 3. Accept choices that are supported by sound reasoning.

ASSESSING PART 3

Use Check-Up 3 (TG page 66) to assess student learning.

NOTE FROM JOY HAKIM

Do you know any sea chanteys? Or railroad songs? Or pioneer ballads? Or spirituals? The nineteenth was a century when everyone sang; it's time we revived that tradition. Your library should have American songbooks and you must have some students who play the guitar or piano—so clear your throat and do some warbling.

PROJECTS AND ACTIVITIES

▶ **Stagecoach Trip**

Have students reread the account of Rebecca Yokum's stagecoach trip in Chapter 14. Then assign groups of students to take the roles of passengers on the coach. Have each group write a conversation that takes place among the passengers. The dialogue should include their reasons for going west and their comments on their journey. Groups may perform their skits for the class.

▶ **A Whale of a Tale**

Ask students to write a short story about a clever whale that is hard to catch. The story may be told in the first person, with them as members of the crew.

▶ **From New England to Japan**

Ask students to use a map of the world to find the latitude and longitude of Japan and New Bedford, Massachusetts. Then ask them to use the map scale to determine the length of Manjiro's journey to America with Captain Whitfield.

▶ **Levis Ad**

Have students look again at the advertisement for Levi's on page 78. What about it appealed to Westerners? Invite groups or individuals to recreate the ad, or design a new one for today.

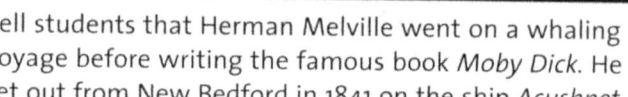
FACTS TO SHARE

Tell students that Herman Melville went on a whaling voyage before writing the famous book *Moby Dick*. He set out from New Bedford in 1841 on the ship *Acushnet*.

INTRODUCING PART 4

Pursuing Progress

In the late 1830s, Captain Frederick Marryat, an English visitor to America, remarked: *"Go ahead is the real motto of the country."* For many people in the United States, progress meant new territories, expanding industries, and growing cities. Part 4 takes a look at some of the changes that helped shape the American belief in progress.

Chapter 18 Cities and Progress, *Student Book page 107*
Chapter 19 A Land of Movers, *Student Book page 112*
Chapter 20 Workin' on the Railroad, *Student Book page 116*

SETTING GOALS

The goals for students in Part 4 are to:
- list problems that faced cities in the mid-19th century.
- describe rural life in Indiana in 1829.
- understand the significance of the Rock Island bridge across the Mississippi River.

GETTING INTERESTED

1. Write *progress* on the chalkboard. Ask what the word means. *(moving forward, change, making improvements, building industries)* Ask students to skim the chapter titles and illustrations in Chapters 18-20. Ask: How was America making progress? *(by building cities, settling new towns, and building railroads, steamboats, and ports)*

2. Ask students to read the caption at the bottom of page 108. Ask: How do new ideas help a nation expand and progress? *(Inventions and technology can improve transportation, communication, and building methods.)*

Working with Timelines
Refer students to page 107 and read aloud the last two paragraphs. Elicit that students can make the generalization that Americans were beginning to move to the cities and that the number of cities in America was increasing. Have students construct a timeline for the decades 1790-1860. Ask them to record the statistics about population growth given in pages 107 and 108 on their timelines.

Using Maps
Have students turn to the Atlas on pages 216-217. Ask them to identify the states in the original United States, and explain that they will be reading about events that occurred in this part of the U.S. in these chapters. Then, using a classroom map of the United States, have students locate the following places mentioned in these chapters: New York City, New Orleans, Louisiana, Indiana, Chicago, Illinois, and the Mississippi River.

PART 4 | 35

TEACHING CHAPTER 18
pages 107-111   1 class period, 35-50 minutes

Cities and Progress

As the 1800s opened, new inventions and machines began to remake America. Nowhere were the changes more noticeable than in the growing cities east of the Mississippi.

ASK

1. What amazing sights would you see if you were a tourist visiting an American city in the mid-1800s? *(tall buildings, fancy hotels, newspapers, department stores with huge display windows, elevators, indoor bathrooms, running water, newspapers)*
2. What problems were caused by the rapid growth of the cities? *(crime; disease; poor sanitation; overcrowded buildings with little air, sunlight, or free space; danger of fire)*
3. Why was *The Sun* read by so many people? *(It only cost one penny so that many people could afford to read it.)*
4. Have students complete Resource 7 (TG page 77) to graph the growth of cities from 1790 to 1860.

Ponder
From 1790 to 1860, Philadelphia grew 25 times larger and New York grew 50 times larger. What do you suppose would happen if your city grew that fast in 70 years?

Question Chart

DISCUSS

1. Tell students that Cincinnati, which had a population of 160,000 in 1860, barely existed as a frontier settlement in 1790. Ask: Why do you think frontier cities like Cincinnati attracted so many people? *(Possible response: People may have moved further west to get away from crowded conditions in the East; many immigrants moved on from the East; Americans were restless and always looking for new opportunities.)*
2. What do you think of the success of John Jacob Astor? *(Responses will vary. He was an amazingly successful immigrant to this country. He seemed to want to buy everything.)*

WRITE

Ask students to work with a partner to prepare a Top Ten list of problems facing the typical American city in the 1840s. Have them present their lists to the class.

LITERACY LINKS

Words to Discuss

technology	know-how
tenement	urban
census	rural

Have students use the dictionary to determine the meaning of each word. Then ask: Which pair of words are antonyms? *(urban, rural)* Which pair of words mean almost the same thing? *(technology, know-how)*. Explain to students that the U.S. government conducts a census every few years, and that they are included in these statistics.

Reading Skills
Analyzing Graphic Aids

Have students preview the chapter by examining the visuals and their captions. Point out that up until now, students have been reading about the expansion of America and trades such as whaling. Ask: What do you predict this chapter will be about? *(cities and buildings; New York City; people who lived in the city)* PREDICTING

Skills Connection
Geography

Name three of the largest U.S. cities in 1860: New York, Chicago, New Orleans. Have students locate them on a wall map. Ask:
- What do these cities' locations have in common? *(Each is located on a river, lake, or ocean.)*
- How might their location have helped these cities grow? *(Water made it possible to transport goods, and trade helped the cities prosper.)*

Have students complete Resource 8 (TG page 78).

36 | LIBERTY FOR ALL?

TEACHING CHAPTER 19 pages 112-115   1 class period, 35-50 minutes

A Land of Movers

Americans saw settlement of the frontier as progress. By the mid-1800s, "progress" had reached the Northwest Territory as wilderness settlements became thriving towns.

ASK

1. Where does Jacob receive his education? *(He goes to a schoolmaster's school, which his parents paid for.)*
2. Who was Jacob's friend Ohiyesa? *(a Shawnee Indian boy)* Why doesn't Ohiyesa live in Indiana any more? *(The settlers crowded out the Shawnee and other Native Americans.)*
3. Why did Ida and her family go to Indiana? *(to escape slavery; so Ida would not be sold)*
4. What changes took place in the Northwest Territory during Jacob's lifetime? *(change from wilderness to settled communities, disappearance of Native Americans, arrival of immigrants)*

DISCUSS

1. Will Jacob and his wife and children do the same kind of work that Jacob's family did when he was a boy? Explain. *(Life will be very different. Inventions like washing and sewing machines mean that women won't need to wash, spin, weave, and make clothing by hand; people will use pumps instead of hauling water, cooking will be easier with Franklin stoves. Jacob became a lawyer and later a state senator.)*
2. The people in Jacob's life were very diverse. Where did some of them come from? *(Jacob's family was German, Ohiyesa was Shawnee, Ida was African American, Jacob's wife was Irish; he probably knew people from other places as well.)*

Ponder
What did people mean when they said the United States was "a melting pot"? Is that still true?

 Question Chart

WRITE

Ask students to write a journal entry entitled "A Day in the Life of Jacob Kessler, Tuesday, April 19, 1829." Fill it with details from Chapter 19. Note that Tuesday is a school day, but there are still the usual chores to be done.

LITERACY LINKS

Words to Discuss

Quaker   sod

Have students look up each word in the dictionary. Ask: Why was sod used as a building material? *(It was easily available.)* How did the Quakers' beliefs lead them to help protect the blacks? *(They believed in peace, which includes fairness between peoples.)*

Reading Skills
Identifying Text Organization

Have students list the houses that Jacob lived in. *(hut, one-room cabin, wood-frame house in town, his own grand house)* Discuss how this progression shows the development of the territory. Help students recognize that the author is using chronological order, although by houses, not by years. ANALYZING

Skills Connection
Geography

Jacob's wife and her family came to America from Ireland and settled in Indiana. Have students look at the world map on pages 214-215 and then at the U.S. map on pages 216-217. Have students list the waterways and states the Kelleys would probably have crossed to reach their destination.

PART 4 | 37

TEACHING CHAPTER 20 pages 116-119   1 class period, 35-50 minutes

Workin' on the Railroad

To many Americans, no invention symbolized progress better than the railroad. In 1856, amid a storm of controversy over which towns would control commerce in the Midwest, the first railroad crossed the Mississippi River on the new Rock Island bridge.

ASK

1. What are two reasons that February 22, 1854 was such an exciting day? *(The first railroad arrived at Rock Island from the East Coast; the date was George Washington's birthday.)*
2. Why might a Mississippi steamboat captain be unhappy about the railroad bridge at Rock Island? *(It might make the river more dangerous to navigate; it might get in the way of the boats; it might take business away from the boats.)*
3. What kind of information did Abraham Lincoln gather to defend the railroad owners against the owners of the *Effie Afton* after it crashed into the bridge? *(information about tides, river currents, the size of the Effie Afton and the bridge, and what the captain had to do to avoid the bridge)*

Ponder
The passengers on the first train to cross the Mississippi were impressed. What trip in your lifetime has excited you the most?

Question Chart

DISCUSS

1. Why was the conflict between railroads and steamboats also a conflict between the North and the South? *(The railroads wanted to link the West to the North by rail to make centers of trade in the North. The steamboats wanted the links to the West to go through the South, and they didn't want to lose business to the North.)*
2. The trial over the *Effie Afton* went all the way to the Supreme Court. What does that suggest about the importance of the case? *(The case was important because the railroad bridge would link lands east of the Mississippi to lands in the West. Railroads were seen as important to progress.)*

WRITE

Ask students which they would have preferred in 1854: a steamboat trip on the Mississippi or a railroad trip on the Chicago and Rock Island line. Have them use information in the chapter to support their opinions.

LITERACY LINKS

Words to Discuss

commerce

Elicit the meaning of *commerce*. Start a word web on the chalkboard with *commerce* at the center. Have students suggest synonyms or related words to fill out the web. *(trade, business, stores, goods, buying, selling, and so on)*

Reading Skills
Recognizing Cause and Effect

Help students recognize the effects of the railroad crossing the Mississippi at Rock Island by asking how it would affect the following items. ANALYZING

- Chicago *(It would become a major trade center.)*
- Steamboats *(They would lose business; trains could transport goods to the East faster.)*
- Trade between the West and the East coast *(It would increase.)*

Skills Connection
History/Economics

Rock Island was identified in 1828 as the best place for a bridge to cross the Mississippi because of the island and the river's narrow channel. Ask students how the new railroad bridge across the river to Davenport would help or hurt the economy of Rock Island. *(People who were traveling might not even get off the train in Rock Island, which could hurt local businesses and ferry owners. But the traffic through Rock Island might also help the economy.)*

38 | LIBERTY FOR ALL?

SUMMARIZING PART 4

THINKING ABOUT THE THEMES

The following questions will help students relate the book's themes to the content of Part 4. You may wish to use these questions for classroom discussion or have students answer them in written form.

1. Suppose the railroads hadn't won the right to cross the Mississippi River. How might the history of the United States have been different? *(Help students predict the important role of the railroad and the expansion of the United States.)*

2. How would you compare and contrast rural life in Indiana and urban life in New York in the mid-1800s? *(Life in Indiana was difficult but seemed to provide opportunities for people to improve their lives; in New York, poor people lived in overcrowded tenements with poor sanitation and crime. Some of those people might emigrate west, if they could.)*

3. Draw students' attention to the other themes that have been posted around the room. Give them the opportunity to explore the relevance of these themes to Part 4. Accept choices that are supported by sound reasoning.

ASSESSING PART 4

Use Check-Up 4 (TG page 67) to assess student learning.

NOTE FROM JOY HAKIM

Are we still a land of movers? Find out. Have each student do a family map tracing the movement of family members inside our country. Then you can give out pins and colored thread and let everyone show that same movement on a big class map–it should end up spider-webbed with many colors.

PROJECTS AND ACTIVITIES

▶ Court Reporters
Assign students to write newspaper stories about the *Effie Afton* court trial. Have students include a headline and answer the five key questions—Who? What? When? Where? Why?

▶ Designing a Poster
Reread the quote from Introducing Part 4 (TG page 35) by Captain Marryat: "*Go ahead* is the real motto of the country." Have students create a poster illustrating the new motto for the United States: *Go Ahead*.

▶ Railroad Songs
Tell students that a song, "The Rock Island Line," first recorded by Huddie Ledbetter, is about the Chicago and Rock Island railroad. Have students write lyrics for a song about the railroad—what rail travel was like and how railroads sparked people's imaginations. Explain that there are hundreds of American railroad folk songs. Students might like to listen to samples of railroad songs at *mcneilmusic.com/railroad.html*.

▶ Ida's Story
Assign students to use the information about Ida in Chapter 19 as the basis for writing a short biography of Ida's life. Students may add details and descriptions of their own, as long as they stick to the facts of Ida's story.

★★ FACTS TO SHARE ★★

Mark Twain, the author of *Tom Sawyer*, grew up in Hannibal, Missouri. In an interview, he said, "Do you know what it means to be a boy on the banks of the Mississippi, to see the steamboats go up and down the river, and never to have had a ride on one? I think not." At 7 years old, he stowed away on a steamboat, only to be discovered and sent home. Twain later become a steamboat pilot, and wrote about it in *Life on the Mississippi*.

INTRODUCING PART 5

Seeking Perfection

In the mid-1800s, some people tried to "re-form" the United States through the expansion of human rights. A number of outspoken women felt that the time had come for them to share the benefits of freedom. As New Englander Margaret Fuller put it in 1843: "As the principle of liberty is better understood and more nobly interpreted, a broader protest [will be] made in behalf of woman . . . ." Part 5 tells about those protests and the conflicts they caused.

Chapter 21 "She Wishes to Ornament Their Minds," *Student Book page 120*
Chapter 22 Do Girls Have Brains?, *Student Book page 125*
Chapter 23 Seneca Falls and the Rights of Women, *Student Book page 130*
Chapter 24 A Woman Named Truth, *Student Book page 136*
Chapter 25 Life in the Mills, *Student Book page 138*
Chapter 26 Working Women and Children, *Student Book page 142*

SETTING GOALS

The goals for students in Part 5 are to:
- list the contributions of early education reformers.
- explain the significance of the Seneca Falls Convention.
- analyze changing attitudes toward women's capabilities.
- describe working conditions for women and children.

GETTING INTERESTED

1. Have students read the chapter titles for Chapters 21-26. Ask: What topics do you think these chapters discuss? *(the struggle for women's rights and decent working conditions)* What are women's rights? *(the right to have the same rights as men)*
2. Draw a timeline on the board with the dates 1776, 1848, 1920, and 1984. After students recognize 1776, write *All men are created equal* below it. Below 1848 write *First women's rights convention*; below 1920 write *Women could vote in national elections*; below 1984 write *First woman nominated for Vice-President*. Ask: Why do you think women had to struggle for their rights? *(They were viewed as being unequal to men; they were not allowed to vote until 1920).* How do you think those rights were established? *(through struggle and reform)*

Working with Timelines
Ask students to draw a 19th-century timeline titled *Human Rights for Women*. They should start the timeline in 1797, the probable year that Sojourner Truth was born, and end it in 1883, the year of her death. Students should take notes as they read, making entries of important dates after each chapter.

Using Maps
Explain that events or documents may be identified with the place that they occurred or were created. Such is the case with Seneca Falls. Help students locate Seneca Falls, New York, on a map (in western New York, near Seneca Lake). Explain that the women's rights convention that took place there in 1848 is still having an effect in our society today.

TEACHING CHAPTER 21   pages 120-124   1 class period, 35-50 minutes

"She Wishes to Ornament Their Minds"

Some 19th-century reformers brought the ideal of universal education within closer reach by opening the doors of schools to women and black Americans.

ASK

1. What kinds of schooling were available to students in the 1830s? *(free public schools, private tutors or private schools, schools built by parents who hired a teacher)*
2. Why did Mary Lyon found Mount Holyoke College? *(She wanted to go to college, but there was no college for women, so she started Mount Holyoke.)*
3. Why did the nation's Founders support the ideal of universal education? *(It promoted self-government and public happiness.)* Why wasn't education mentioned in the Constitution? *(The founders expected the states to control schooling.)*
4. Have students use Resource 9 (TG page 79) to tackle a lesson from *McGuffey's Reader*.

Ponder
What would this country be like if public education had not been established here?

 **Question Chart**

DISCUSS

1. What contributions did Noah Webster make to American education? *(He wrote American schoolbooks, a spelling book, and an American dictionary.)* Why do you think it was important for Americans to have their own schoolbooks, and not British books? *(American books would tell about the country's history, people, and experiences, and use American English.)*
2. What did a student mean by saying that the founder of Litchfield Academy wished to "ornament" womens' minds? *(She wanted them to have intellectual skills as well as skills such as needlework.)*
3. How did churches influence education? *(Some people learned to read in Sunday school and read Bible stories.)*

WRITE

George Washington said: "Knowledge is, in every country, the surest basis of public happiness." Have students write a brief paragraph explaining what Washington meant.

LITERACY LINKS

Words to Discuss

universal   college
academy   seminary
finishing school

Have students use a dictionary to determine the meaning of each term. Then write the heading *Education* on the chalkboard. Elicit from students types of schools mentioned in the text, and write them on the board. Include other types of schools students can name.

Reading Skills
Interpreting Point of View

Sourcebook Have volunteers read aloud Horace Mann's report (Source #41). Elicit from students why Mann feels that universal education is essential to the success of a country with a republican form of government. ANALYZING

Skills Connection
Geography

Ask students to comment on the truth of this generalization: "In America, education reform started in the East and worked its way west." *(It is true; Pierce, Webster, Lyon, and Mann were all from Connecticut or Massachusetts.)* Why do you think this was true? *(The communities in the East were older; they had time to develop institutions such as schools; people in the West were busy settling the frontier.)*

PART 5 | 41

TEACHING CHAPTER 22   pages 125-129   1 class period, 35-50 minutes

Do Girls Have Brains?

Common ideas about the inferiority of women were challenged in the mid-1800s by women who dared enter public forums and fields once reserved for men.

ASK

1. Why did few people know about the accomplishments of Phillis Wheatley and Lucy Prince? *(History books were written by men who believed that women were not as smart or as important as men, and so the women were left out.)*
2. How could a husband control his wife? *(He could whip her, he owned all the woman's money or property, he could take the children if the wife left.)*
3. Why did some people call the Grimké sisters "monster women"? *(They felt it was unnatural and irreligious for women to speak out in front of men, and the Grimkés spoke in front of many crowds.)*

Ponder
In colleges in the 1800s, female students could not read their papers aloud; male professors had to read them. How did that made the females feel?

Question Chart

DISCUSS

1. Discrimination can be said to hurt all people. Why? *(It leads to unfair treatment of people; it deprives people of their rights; it doesn't allow people to make contributions that would benefit society.)*
2. What about the marriage of Henry Blackwell and Lucy Stone seems modern to you? *(They were equal partners in the marriage; Lucy Stone refused to give up her legal identity and the right to her own property.)*

WRITE

Have students choose one of the women mentioned in the chapter. In a paragraph about the woman, they should tell why she is worthy of admiration.

LITERACY LINKS

Words to Discuss

antislavery   rational

Have students determine the meaning of *rational* from context. Elicit that *anti-* is a prefix that means "opposed to," and have students tell the meaning of *antislavery*.

Reading Skills
Using Primary Sources

Use the Just a Joke feature on page 128 to help students understand the uses of a primary source.
CONNECTING

- What were Blackwell's feelings on November 15? *(She was sad and discouraged.)* How had her feelings changed by November 24? *(She was joyful; she would be included in all the activities.)*

- Why do you know more of her experience than if someone else wrote about it? *(She gives a firsthand account of what happened.)*

Skills Connection
Folk Art

Explain that some of the richest historical sources are the folk art and domestic arts of everyday people. Ask students to read the lines from the sewing sampler on page 125. Have them compose a sampler for today instructing women and men how "to give domestic life its sweetest charm."

TEACHING CHAPTER 23
pages 130-135 · 1 class period, 35-50 minutes

Seneca Falls and the Rights of Women

The desire for equality led women to climb new mountains—from tackling female suffrage to scaling Pikes Peak. One of the high points was the Seneca Falls Convention—a meeting that gave birth to the women's rights movement.

ASK

1. How did Elizabeth Cady Stanton learn the law? *(from her father, who was a judge, and from studying on her own)*
2. What was the purpose of the Seneca Falls Declaration? *(to demand equality and to state the injustices faced by women)*
3. Who supported the Seneca Falls Declaration *(anti-slavery papers, Frederick Douglass, some women who signed)* Why did some women who signed the declaration remove their names from it? *(The public pressure against the declaration was very great.)*

DISCUSS

1. What about the marriage ceremony (customary at the time) did Elizabeth Cady Stanton object to? Why? *(She said that she would not "obey" her husband; she insisted that she was entering into the marriage as an equal.)*
2. **Sourcebook** Read aloud from Source #42 as students follow along. List on the chalkboard Stanton's topics: intellectual superiority, moral superiority, physical superiority. Have students name important points in Stanton's arguments and list them under each topic.
3. **Sourcebook** Read aloud from Source #43 as students follow along. Ask: How did the Seneca Falls Declaration change these famous words from the Declaration of Independence: "all men are created equal"? *("all men *and women* are created equal")*

WRITE

Have students make up posters advertising the Seneca Falls Convention. They should tell the purpose of the gathering, and why people should attend.

Ponder
Are you looking forward to when you are old enough to vote? What issues will concern you then?

 **Question Chart**

LITERACY LINKS

Words to Discuss
reform

Have partners create a 2-column chart with the words *reform* (noun), *reform* (verb), and *reformer* (noun) in the first column, and the definition for each word in the second column.

Reading Skills
Evaluating Point of View

Help students analyze the author's point of view about the women's movement. ANALYZING

- What is the author's point of view about the women's movement? (She is in favor of it
- How do you know? *(Hakim's tone is very positive when she describes the activities of the leaders of the women's movement.)*

Meeting Individual Needs
Reteaching

Have students create a two-column chart to keep track of the reformers mentioned in this chapter. In the left column they should write the name of each person, and in the right column they should write what the person did.

PART 5 | 43

TEACHING CHAPTER 24
pages 136-137 · 1 class period, 35-50 minutes

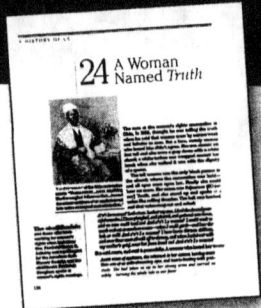

A Woman Named *Truth*

Abolition and the struggle for women's rights were joined in the electrifying person of Sojourner Truth, an African American crusader who spent her life pursuing the ideal of justice.

ASK

1. Why did Sojourner Truth stand up and speak at the women's rights convention in Ohio? *(She couldn't stand it that a man was saying women were weak and inferior to men.)*
2. What does *sojourner* mean? *(a traveler who stops briefly and then moves on)* When Isabella changed her name to Sojourner Truth, what did she announce about her goals? *(She intended to travel in pursuit of truth and justice.)*
3. Besides women's rights, what causes did Sojourner Truth fight for? *(abolition of slavery, prison reform, and temperance)*

Ponder Sojourner Truth chose her name to say something about her life. What name would you choose for yourself?

Question Chart

DISCUSS

1. **Sourcebook** Read aloud from Source #46 as students follow along. Then ask: What was Sojourner Truth's message in the "A'n't I a Woman" speech? *(to establish that she has a physical strength and an emotional strength equal to that of a man)* How does this combat the idea that men are naturally superior to women? *(If one woman can do these things, other women can, too. There is no natural reason that one sex is superior to the other sex.)*
2. How did Truth manage to get back one of her children who had been resold into slavery? *(With the help of some Quakers, she found a lawyer, went to court, and got her child back.)* What does this say about her character? *(She was determined, didn't accept injustice, and wasn't afraid to be involved in the legal system to effect change.)*

WRITE

Abraham Lincoln asked Sojourner Truth to come to the White House. Have students compose the letter Lincoln may have written, inviting her to visit him and his family.

LITERACY LINKS

Words to Discuss

abolitionist   sojourner
feminist

Point out that all three words are made up of a base word and a suffix. Have students identify the word parts and use them to define the words. *(abolition-ist: one who believes in abolishing slavery; femin-ist: one who believes in feminism; sojourn-er: one who travels with long stays in different places.)*

Reading Skills
Recognizing Rhetorical Devices

Have students identify the phrase in Truth's speech (page 136) that is repeated several times. *(A'n't I a woman?)* Explain that repetition is a device that speechmakers often use. Ask why Sojourner repeats this phrase. *(It emphasizes her ideas and makes the line memorable.)* How do these words help create an image in the listener's mind? *(The listener sees a strong woman saying these words.)*
VISUALIZING

Skills Connection
History

It might surprise students that Sojourner was a slave in New York in 1826. Although some northern states abolished slavery during or right after the Revolution, slavery continued in New York until 1827 and was not entirely abolished in New Jersey until 1846. Have students begin a timeline about slavery and abolition using these facts. They can add to their timelines as they complete this book.

44 | LIBERTY FOR ALL?

TEACHING CHAPTER 25
pages 138-141 1 class period, 35-50 minutes

Life in the Mills

Industrial growth brought economic opportunity for men and women. But it also brought child labor and the creation of "wage slaves" trapped in unhealthy factories, mills, and mines.

ASK

1. What problems of industry did Rebecca Harding write about? *(dangers and unhealthy conditions for ironworkers)*
2. What two kinds of people lived in Wheeling, where Rebecca Harding lived? *(wealthy people and ironworkers)* Why was Harding's *Life in the Iron Mills* so significant and unusual? *(No one had written before about wage slaves; Harding wrote about the ironworkers in Wheeling; people who were not wage slaves were unaware of labor conditions.)*

DISCUSS

1. The author says that the people who worked in the factories, mines, and mills were also "slaves." What does she mean? *(Their lives were horrible; their working conditions were terrible; they were without hope; they were not free to change their lives.)*
2. Why do you think workers in the factories, mines, and mills stayed and worked in such terrible conditions? *(They needed the money to live and had no way to find other work.)*
3. Have students complete Resource 10 (TG page 80) to gain understanding about worker's hours, wages, and expenses.

WRITE

Have students write a paragraph describing the most difficult physical work they have ever done. For how long did they have to do it? Did it give them any satisfaction? What would have made it easier? Have volunteers share their stories.

Ponder
Are working conditions in factories, mines, and mills better today than in the past? How have they improved?

Question Chart

LITERACY LINKS

Words to Discuss

labor union   strike
valedictorian

Have students find definitions for the words in a dictionary. Then ask them to write a sentence that includes the words *labor union* and *strike*. Ask: What would cause laborers to strike?

Reading Skills
Evaluating Visual Aids

Have students scan the illustrations and photographs in this chapter. Lead them in discovering the mood these visual aids present about industrial work in the mid-1800s. *(The mood is dark and gloomy.)* Elicit the details that create this mood. *(dangerous, difficult labor; polluted air; dark mines; child labor)* ANALYZING

Skills Connection
Geography

Wheeling, Virginia, was on the National Road. Provide students with a U.S. road atlas, and let them trace the route of the National Road, which is followed by the present U.S. Route 40. Explain that the National Road was also known as the Cumberland Road, because it started at Cumberland, Maryland, and ran westward to St. Louis, Missouri.

PART 5 | 45

TEACHING CHAPTER 26 pages 142-146 1 class period, 35-50 minutes

Working Women and Children

Wage-earning women in the United States outnumbered working women in Europe. They faced wretched conditions that writer Herman Melville felt made them little better than "cogs to the wheel."

ASK

1. Why were so many women and children hired to work in factories? *(They worked for lower wages than men did.)*
2. What kinds of jobs did women have in America that they didn't have in Europe? *(blacksmiths, shoemakers, barrel makers, and teachers)*

Ponder
How did labor laws concerning children change?

 **Question Chart**

DISCUSS

1. Why do you think children were paid even less than women, even though they did the same kinds of jobs? *(They were young and couldn't fight for better pay; being completely dependent, they did what they were told by adults to do.)*
2. Have students complete Resource 11 (TG page 81) to appreciate how the timetable of Lowell Mills ordered workers' lives.

WRITE

Ask students to select a photograph or illustration from Chapter 26 and write a new caption for it. The caption should give information about the working conditions in the mills.

LITERACY LINKS

Words to Discuss

textile mill
assembly line

Ask students to name the root word of *assembly*. *(assemble)* Ask them to use context clues to infer the meaning of "assembly line" and then have them check their definitions in the dictionary. Ask: What might be some steps on an assembly line that makes cars? That makes computers?

Reading Skills
Evaluating Author's Perspective

Have students compare Paul's letter, Melville's description, and Tubman's words on pages 144-146. Discuss that each talks about "slave" work, but that Paul says positive things about the conditions, whereas the other two are negative. Elicit reasons for each person's perspective. ANALYZING

Skills Connection
Geography

Elicit from students why mills were usually situated along rivers. *(Flowing water powered the mills' machines.)* Explain that the fast-moving rivers in the North were better suited for this than the slower-moving rivers in the South, which was one reason why the North industrialized so quickly. Ask students to locate Lowell, Massachusetts, on a map (northwest of Boston) and note its location on the Merrimack River.

46 | LIBERTY FOR ALL?

SUMMARIZING PART 5

THINKING ABOUT THE THEMES

The following questions will help students relate the book's themes to the content of Part 5. You may wish to use these questions for classroom discussion or have students answer them in written form.

1. By 1860, in what areas had women made some progress in the struggle for their rights? *(Women made gains in education by creating schools and colleges for women; they began to speak out and be heard on women's issues in forums like the Seneca Falls convention.)*

2. What was the state of women and children's rights in the workplace in the 1860s? *(There were no laws that protected them; they worked in terrible conditions for very little money.)*

3. What were some of the reasons that the abolitionist and women's rights movements were linked? *(Many women in the women's rights movement, believing in rights for all people, were also against slavery; Sojourner Truth became a spokeswoman for both issues.)*

4. Draw students' attention to the other themes that have been posted around the room. Give them the opportunity to explore the relevance of these themes to Part 5. Accept choices that are supported by sound reasoning.

ASSESSING PART 1

Use Check-Up 5 (TG page 68) to assess student learning.

NOTE FROM JOY HAKIM

Some school news: Mrs. Carl Shurz, who studied the kindergarten movement in Germany, organized the first American kindergarten in 1855 in Watertown, Wisconsin. All the children spoke German. That same year, Henry Barnard of Connecticut published the American Journal of Education. It helped give professional status to those who were making teaching a career. Barnard was the first U.S. commissioner of education.

PROJECTS AND ACTIVITIES

▶ Create an Advertisement

Ask students to select one of the following people: Sarah Pierce, Mary Lyon, Emma Willard, or Horace Mann. Have students work in groups to design newspaper advertisements announcing a new school started by that particular reformer. The ad should mention how the school will change education.

▶ Write a Review for a Dictionary

Assign students to write a newspaper review of Noah Webster's new dictionary. The review should mention some of the "Americanisms" included in the dictionary and give reasons Americans might want to buy a copy of the dictionary.

▶ Hold a Press Conference

Have volunteers play the parts of the following reformers: Angelina and Sarah Grimké, Elizabeth Blackwell, Lucy Stone, Elizabeth Cady Stanton, Susan B. Anthony, and Amelia Bloomer. Other students should role-play reporters and write interview questions that they might ask during a press conference.

▶ Write Song Lyrics

Have students write additional lyrics for the mill girl's song on page 8 of the textbook. How has her liberty been affected? What kind of life does she wish for? Students may wish to set their lyrics to a familiar song.

★★ FACTS TO SHARE ★★

Although children were employed in U.S. factories from the time that Samuel Slater built the first American factory in 1789, no serious national regulation of child labor occurred until the 1930s. In 1938, the federal Wages and Hours Act banned employment of children under the age of 16 by companies engaged in interstate commerce (although allowing certain instances of employment of 14-16-year-olds). That is the basic law still followed today.

INTRODUCING PART 6

Creating a National Identity

In 1837, American poet, essayist, and philosopher Ralph Waldo Emerson delivered a speech at Harvard which declared America's cultural independence. He said, "We will walk on our own feet; we will work with our own hands; we will speak our own minds." Part 6 tells about the writers and artists who helped describe America.

Chapter 27 American Writers, *Student Book page 147*
Chapter 28 Mr. Thoreau–at Home with the World, *Student Book page 150*
Chapter 29 Melville and Company, *Student Book page 152*
Chapter 30 If a Poet Writes You a Letter, Pay Attention, *Student Book page 156*
Chapter 31 Painter of Birds and Painter of Indians, *Student Book page 162*

SETTING GOALS

The goals for students in Part 6 are to:
- name prominent American writers and painters of the 1830s-1850s.
- explain why Thoreau is one of America's greatest thinkers.
- explain the significance of Audubon and Catlin in preserving the national heritage.

GETTING INTERESTED

1. Write the title of Part 6 on the chalkboard. Ask: What is a person's identity? *(the condition of being a particular person, or the sense of being different from other people)* What is a national identity? *(a country's particular characteristics)* Where did the United States get its national identity from? *(different kinds of people developing common values, struggling with common enemies, experiencing common hardships, aspiring to common ideals, sharing a common history)*

2. Refer students to the Tales That Are Whoppers Are Tall feature on page 155 and ask volunteers to read it aloud. Ask: How did tall tales become part of America's cultural identity? *(Tall tales are stories about ordinary people who did extraordinary things—unlike European stories that were usually about privileged people or fairy tales.)*

Working with Timelines
As students read about the writers and artists in this part, have them list the name of each artist, the work, and the date (or approximate date) that the work was created. As they make additions, have them cross-reference their list with the timeline they created in Part 5 to see which reformers may have read, seen, or been influenced by these artists and writers.

Using Maps
Read the opening sentence of Chapter 27 *(New England was different)* and have students locate the New England states on the classroom wall map. Remind students that the Puritans settled in New England and that some of the effects of Puritanism include strict morality, sense of duty, the importance of education, and a serious attitude about life. Discuss how these traits might affect literature and art from New England.

48 | LIBERTY FOR ALL?

TEACHING CHAPTER 27 pages 147-149   1 class period, 35-50 minutes

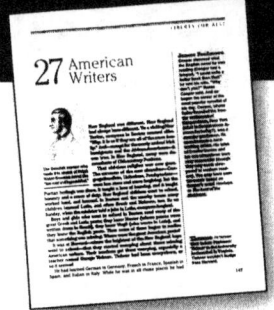

American Writers

The generations that founded American literature grew up as American citizens. They thought and wrote about national achievements—not about colonial or European achievements.

ASK

1. What were some of the values that New Englanders inherited from the Puritans? *(love of learning, honesty, sense of duty)*
2. How did George Ticknor influence the new American literature that came out of New England? *(He encouraged his students at Harvard to write their own stories.)*
3. Why didn't the author of *Little Women* go to Harvard? *(Louisa May Alcott was a woman, and women weren't admitted to Harvard.)*
4. Have students add information about New England writers to Resource 12 (TG page 82).

DISCUSS

1. What languages did children in Boston learn? *(Latin, Greek, and Hebrew)* What languages did George Ticknor know? *(German, French, Spanish, Italian)* Why might it be helpful for a writer to be able to read books in other languages? *(Responses will vary. A writer would be able to read about experiences of people from other lands, appreciate a different language and literature—all of which could help a writer's craft.)*
2. Emerson called the first shot fired in the American Revolution "the shot heard round the world." What did he mean by that? *(Ordinary people were rebelling against those who ruled them; they were fighting for the right to govern themselves. The ideas of freedom and democracy would spread around the world.)*

WRITE

Have students compose a letter to one of the writers mentioned in the chapter, asking him or her to contribute an article for publication in the class newspaper. Include in the letter several topics from which the writer can choose.

Ponder
Which of these writers would you most like to have met?

Question Chart

LITERACY LINKS

Words to Discuss

heritage   **sage**

Have students define these words from context and write sentences using the words. Point out that the noun *sage* is a homograph—a word that is spelled like another but has a different meaning. Which meaning of *sage* is used in this chapter? *(a person who is very wise)*

Reading Skills
Interpreting Word Choice

Read aloud Emerson's "Fable" (page 149). Help students analyze the poem. ANALYZING

- Who is arguing? *(a squirrel and a mountain)*
- What is the meaning of "If I'm not so large as you, / You are not so small as I"? *(Being big is not necessarily better than being small.)*
- What is the main idea of the poem? *(Everything in nature has its place; everyone has his or her own worth.)*

Meeting Individual Needs
Reteaching

Reread with students "Fable" on page 149. Explain unfamiliar vocabulary and demonstrate how following the punctuation by pausing at the commas and stopping at the semicolons and periods helps separate the ideas of the poem. Make sure students appreciate the poem's main point: everything and everyone in nature has value.

PART 6 | 49

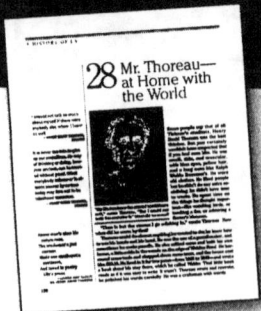

TEACHING CHAPTER 28 pages 150-151   1 class period, 35-50 minutes

Mr. Thoreau—at Home with the World

It was the writer and thinker Henry David Thoreau who best expressed the honesty and individualism of the New England school of writers of the mid-1800s.

ASK

1. What was Henry David Thoreau like? *(He was a great thinker, wore old clothes, didn't socialize, treasured his time and loved nature.)*
2. Where did Thoreau write his book *Walden*? *(on Walden Pond, in Concord, Massachusetts)* What was the subject of the book? *(It was about his two-year-stay in a house he built by himself next to Walden Pond.)*
3. Why was Thoreau put into jail? *(for refusing to pay a tax)* What was Thoreau protesting? *(slavery and the war in Mexico)*
4. Have students add information about Thoreau to Resource 12 (TG page 82).

Ponder
Has there been a time in your life when passive resistance would have worked?

Question Chart

DISCUSS

1. What is the subject of Henry David Thoreau's essay *Civil Disobedience*? *(nonviolent protest: that each person counts when they stand up for freedom; passive resistance—not fighting but not cooperating—when attacked)*
2. In America, are people allowed to practice civil disobedience? *(yes)* Do you think all governments have given people this right? *(No, in countries ruled by dictators, people do not have this right.)*
3. **Sourcebook** Read aloud paragraphs 2 and 3 of Source #44 as students follow along. Have students name the reasons why Thoreau thought it was disgraceful to be associated with the government, and how he proposed that a peaceable revolution might be carried out.

WRITE

Ask students to choose a quotation by Thoreau from the chapter. Then have them write a brief paragraph explaining the quote's meaning in their own words. They can use what they have learned about Thoreau to help them interpret the quote.

LITERACY LINKS

Words to Discuss

civil disobedience
passive resistance

Have students define these words from context. Discuss circumstances under which civil disobedience or passive resistance is the right response.

Reading Skills
Using Text Features

Before students read the chapter, have them skim the text in the margin notes. Preview the chapter.
QUESTIONING

- Who is mentioned in each note? *(Henry David Thoreau)*
- Does Thoreau seem to be more of a celebrity or a thinker? *(a thinker)*

Have partners make up two questions that they would like to have answered about Thoreau.

Meeting Individual Needs
Auditory Learners

Read aloud the quotations by Thoreau in the margin notes, the picture caption on page 150, and the caption to the sketch on page 151. With students, discuss the meaning of each quote, sentence by sentence, if necessary. After students comprehend the quotations, ask volunteers to read aloud one or two of the quotes.

TEACHING CHAPTER 29
pages 152-155 • 1 class period, 35-50 minutes

Melville and Company

Writers in the mid-1800s were inspired by the diversity of the American experience. Melville, Hawthorne, Poe, Cooper, Irving, and Whitman are still important figures in American literary history.

ASK

1. Where did Herman Melville get his education? *(on a whaling ship)* What is his book *Moby Dick* about? *(It is the story of a white whale named Moby Dick and Captain Ahab's determination to catch it.)*
2. What subjects did Washington Irving and Edgar Allan Poe write about? *(Irving: tales from New York's past; Poe: horror stories)*
3. What did Melville, Irving, and James Fenimore Cooper have in common? *(They all had lived in New York.)*
4. Why did Ralph Waldo Emerson call Walt Whitman "the poet of democracy?" *(Whitman wrote about ordinary things and people; he wrote in an "American voice.")* What Whitman poem was he talking about? *(Leaves of Grass)*
5. Have students add the New York writers to Resource 12 (TG page 82).

Ponder
Who in modern times would be a good subject for a tall tale?

 **Question Chart**

DISCUSS

1. Why did critics dislike Walt Whitman's *Leaves of Grass*? *(It was very long, and it didn't rhyme.)* Why do you think people often find it hard to appreciate new ways of writing, painting, or doing things? *(Responses will vary. It is easier to appreciate things that you're familiar with.)*
2. Why could tall tales be called an American art form? *(They were about Americans and they were invented in America.)*

WRITE

Edgar Allan Poe wrote scary stories. Have students write a letter to Poe, suggesting an idea for a new story. They should include the basic idea of the tale and give some details for Poe to use.

LITERACY LINKS

Words to Discuss

tall tale   **rollicking**

Ask students to make a word web for *tall tale*. Have small groups brainstorm words that characterize tall tales to complete the web *(hero, exaggeration, larger-than-life, whopper, and so on)*. Ask students if they know any tall tales. Do they know any tale they would describe as "rollicking"?

Reading Skills
Evaluating Word Choice

Have students concentrate on how the author writes about Whitman. Ask volunteers to list on the chalkboard descriptive words and phrases.
VISUALIZING

- How does the choice of words tell you what she thinks of Whitman? *(The words tell of Whitman's energy; they show respect.)*
- What mental image of Whitman do the descriptions form? *(They bring to mind a lively, enthusiastic person.)*

Skills Connection
Geography

Have students use a globe or the classroom wall map to find the places to which Melville sailed: England, Cape Horn, Hawaii, and Tahiti. Then have them use the classroom map to locate Poe's birthplace, Boston, and then New York (where Whitman, Irving, and Cooper lived).

PART 6 | 51

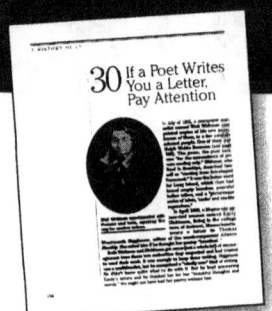

TEACHING CHAPTER 30
pages 156-161 • 1 class period, 35-50 minutes

If a Poet Writes You a Letter, Pay Attention

Emily Dickinson and Walt Whitman could not have been more different. Yet, together they created a fresh, new American voice in poetry.

ASK

1. Who was Emily Dickinson and where did she live? *(a poet who wrote in the 1860s, lived in Amherst, Massachusetts)*
2. What was Dickinson's life like? *(She hardly left the house; she visited Boston only twice.)*
3. How are Whitman and Dickinson judged today? *(They are considered two of America's greatest poets.)*
4. Have students add Dickinson and Whitman to Resource 12 (TG page 82).

Ponder
What is Dickinson saying about fame in poem #1763?

 **Question Chart**

DISCUSS

1. Were Whitman and Dickinson widely read during their lifetimes? Explain. *(Dickinson published only 8 out of her 1,800 poems; Whitman's poems were published, but few people read them.)*
2. How were Whitman's and Dickinson's poems different from other 19th-century poetry? *(They didn't follow the rules of meter, rhyme, and punctuation.)*
3. Have students complete Resource 13 (TG page 83) to analyze "I Hear America Singing" by Walt Whitman.

WRITE

Have students choose one of the poems in the chapter. Ask them to write a brief paragraph expressing their ideas and feelings about it.

LITERACY LINKS

Words to Discuss

meter   recluse

Have students define *recluse* from context. Explain that *meter* is the rhythm in poetry; it's determined by the number and types of beats (pattern of stressed and unstressed syllables) in each line. Encourage students to read the poems aloud. Point out that that's the best way to hear the meter.

Reading Skills
Interpreting Poetry

Explain that "Beat! Beat! Drums!" was one of a group of poems Whitman published in 1865 in reaction to the Civil War, during which the poet worked as a volunteer hospital nurse in Washington. After students read the poem, help them interpret its meaning. INFERRING

- What do the drumbeats and bugles represent? *(announcements of war)*
- Who is affected by war? *(everyone)*
- How are people's lives interrupted? *(People can't continue in their usual roles or professions.)*

Meeting Individual Needs
Kinesthetic Learners

Have students read a poem aloud slowly. They may act out words or phrases to reinforce what is happening in the poem.

52 | LIBERTY FOR ALL?

TEACHING CHAPTER 31
pages 162-170 · 1 class period, 35-50 minutes

Painter of Birds and Painter of Indians

In the mid-1800s, before the invention of photography, it was up to painters to record what America looked like. The paintings of two of the best artists—John James Audubon and George Catlin—captured the diversity of America's people and land.

ASK

1. What inspired John James Audubon to take his drawing seriously? *(He met the ornithologist Alexander Wilson who said his bird paintings were America's best; Audubon knew he could do better.)*
2. What was unusual about the way Audubon drew birds and other animals? *(He drew them in great detail and as they appeared in nature.)*
3. What event in his mother's life inspired Catlin to paint Native Americans? *(She had been captured by Iroquois, treated well, and then released.)*

DISCUSS

1. Why did both Audubon and Catlin feel it was very important to paint the wildlife and people who were their subjects? *(Audubon knew that some animal species wouldn't survive the settlement of the frontier; Catlin knew that both Indians and buffalo were in danger of extinction.)*
2. What kinds of folk art were produced by ordinary people? *(useful items like quilts and yarn reels; items that marked deaths or events in people's lives)*

WRITE

Have students examine the pictures on pages 166-167. Which artist would they have chosen to paint scenes of *their* life? Have students write a letter to the artist of their choice, indicating the particular people and scenes that they would like portrayed.

Ponder
If you were having your portrait painted, would you want the artist to show you sitting, standing, or doing something?

 Question Chart

LITERACY LINKS

Words to Discuss

ornithologist   portrait
engraving   folk art

Have students use context to define the words. Discuss that *folk art* is usually described as art made by everyday people, or people with no formal training. From folk art, we can learn about the skills and interests of people in the past. People's hobbies—such as whittling or needlework—sometimes is considered folk art. What examples of folk art do you see today?

Reading Skills
Comparing and Contrasting

The author presents many points of comparison between Audubon and Catlin. Have partners create a two-column compare-contrast chart for *Audubon* and *Catlin*. Points of comparison should include *Early Life, Early Adulthood, Subject, Painting Style, Accomplishments*. After partners complete the chart, ask: In what ways were the two painters the same? In what ways were they different? SYNTHESIZING

Meeting Individual Needs
Visual Learners

Have students describe the details and the settings of Audubon's paintings and the colors and subjects of Catlin's paintings. Then have them examine the items on pages 168-169. Ask: Do you see any similarities between these works and those of today's artists and craftspeople? Explain that the natural style of Catlin and Audubon, new for its time, is still popular today.

PART 6 | 53

SUMMARIZING PART 6

THINKING ABOUT THE THEMES

The following questions will help students relate the book's themes to the content of Part 6. You may wish to use these questions for classroom discussion or have students answer them in written form.

1. Explain why the mid-1800s was a time of great growth for American literature. *(There was a spurt of American writers who produced works of high quality; the writers wrote about American themes or set their stories in America. Many of these works were read in other countries.)*

2. How did painters like John James Audubon and George Catlin help establish America's identity and preserve its heritage? *(They painted the wildlife and people of America in their natural settings. Some of their subjects were in danger of becoming extinct; when painted, they were preserved for history.)*

3. Draw students' attention to the other themes that have been posted around the room. Give them the opportunity to explore the relevance of these themes to Part 6. Accept choices that are supported by sound reasoning.

ASSESSING PART 6

Use Check-Up 6 (TG page 69) to assess student learning.

PROJECTS AND ACTIVITIES

▶ Mapping the Writers

Have students work in groups to create a large map of the New England states, including states just to the south and west of New England. Using pushpins, students can locate the cities and towns on the map that are associated with the writers in this chapter. Using string, have them connect the locations to index cards that contain the names and works of the writer(s) associated with the place.

▶ Write a Poem

Have students write a poem about an aspect of American life they have read about in this book. Their poems may or may not have a regular rhyming pattern. For inspiration, some students may wish to visit **www.poets.org** to find copies of Walt Whitman's poems.

▶ 19th-Century Art Exhibit

Have students study the pictures in Part 6 and additional works found in library references. They can work in small groups to create a bulletin board exhibit of American drawings and paintings from the 1800s. Groups should organize their exhibits around a theme; for example, "American Wilderness" or "American Portraits." Students can photocopy reproductions in the book, date them (as far as possible), and include the artists' name.

▶ Responding to Emerson

Ask students to choose one of the following statements made by Ralph Waldo Emerson. Have students explain its main idea, tell whether the student agrees or disagrees with the statement, and then give their reasons why.
- "The less government we have the better."
- "Life is too short to waste."
- "The reward of a thing well done, is to have done it."

★★ FACTS TO SHARE ★★

When Walt Whitman's brother was wounded in the Battle of Fredericksburg during the Civil War, Whitman went to Washington to search for him. While in Washington, Whitman took a job as a civil servant. When a civil service official discovered that Whitman was the author of *Leaves of Grass*, he fired him. The official didn't like the book.

INTRODUCING PART 7

Challenging Slavery

Frederick Douglass, the great abolitionist and a former slave, spoke these words to a crowd in 1857: "This struggle may be a moral one; or it may be a physical one; or it may be both moral and physical; but it must be a struggle. Power concedes nothing without a demand." As the 1850s drew to a close, compromise, which had saved the Union time and again, finally broke down. Part 7 traces the conflict over slavery and the build-up to the Civil War.

Chapter 32 *Amistad* Means Friendship, *Student Book page 171*
Chapter 33 Webster Defends the Union, *Student Book page 177*
Chapter 34 Big Problems and a Little Giant, *Student Book page 180*
Chapter 35 A Dreadful Decision, *Student Book page 186*
Chapter 36 Fleeing to Freedom, *Student Book page 188*
Chapter 37 Over the River and Underground, *Student Book page 191*
Chapter 38 Seven Decades, *Student Book page 196*

SETTING GOALS

The goals for students in Part 7 are to:
- understand the implications of the story of the *Amistad*.
- state the key provisions of the Compromise of 1850.
- describe the verdict and the thinking behind the Dred Scott decision.
- explain the workings of the Underground Railroad.
- identify the promise, the problem, and the paradox of America.

GETTING INTERESTED

1. Write the title of Book 5 on the chalkboard. Ask: Why is there a question mark at the end of the title? *(It was questionable whether all Americans enjoyed liberty between 1820 and 1860.)* What groups in the mid-1800s were denied their liberty or their rights? *(women, enslaved Africans, immigrants, Native Americans, the handicapped and mentally ill)*
2. Have students skim the remaining pages in the book to look at the illustrations and headlines. Ask: What kinds of people were involved in the struggle over slavery? *(Africans, whites, politicians)* Where was the struggle taking place? *(all over the United States)* What does this suggest about the conflict over slavery? *(It was a major conflict that touched everybody.)*

Working with Timelines
Ask partners to record significant events and dates about the struggle over slavery on individual index cards. Explain that these events are important, as they tell about what happened in the years before the Civil War. After reading all of the chapters, students can sequence their cards in time order and use them to review the events in Part 6. They can also complete Resource 14 (TG page 84).

Using Maps
Have students turn to the map on page 182 and read its title and labels. Then have students use the classroom wall map of the United States (or the map on page 216) to determine the names of the present-day states that were included in the "Free States and Territories" and "Slave States and Territories."

PART 7 | 55

TEACHING CHAPTER 32
pages 171-176 1 class period, 35-50 minutes

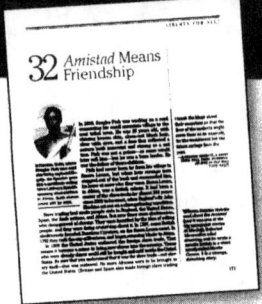

Amistad Means Friendship

Africans resisted enslavement. No event proved this more dramatically than the slave revolt aboard the slave ship *Amistad*.

ASK

1. Where was Sengbe Pieh captured? *(Sierra Leone, Africa)* What terrible ordeals did he face after his capture? *(loss of his family, wretched journey aboard a slave ship, sale in a slave market, and so on)*
2. Why did the slavers change Sengbe Pieh's name to Joseph Cinque? *(to cover up the fact that they had broken laws banning the foreign slave trade)*
3. What principles did John Quincy Adams use to defend the Africans who mutinied on the *Amistad*? *(He used the principles in the Declaration of Independence that upheld the right to rebel when human rights are violated.)*

Ponder
Why isn't a novel the best source for learning history?

Question Chart

DISCUSS

1. What were the basic facts of the *Amistad* case that went before the courts? *(The Africans were illegally captured and sold into slavery. The people who did that broke U.S., British, and Spanish laws.)* What were the political issues involved? *(Blacks had mutinied and killed whites, which slave owners feared. Blacks were fighting for their freedom, which is what abolitionists had been waiting for. Spain protested that a Spanish ship was captured. The British might invade Cuba.)*
2. What does it mean that the slave trade, but not slavery, was outlawed in the United States? *(New slaves were not allowed to be brought to the U.S., but people who were already slaves, or the children of slaves, were still enslaved.)*
3. At the last trial of Cinque and his fellow Africans, the judge was not an abolitionist. How come he set them free? *(He respected the law, which was more important than his personal feelings. And the law, which prohibited the slave trade, had been broken.)*

WRITE

Have students suppose they were present at the *Amistad* trial. Ask them to write, in their own words, the main ideas of what John Quincy Adams said in his speech to the court.

LITERACY LINKS

Words to Discuss

emancipate   slaver
mutiny   gag rule

Have students use context to write the definition of each word. Ask: Which word would an abolitionist use? *(emancipate)* Where does a mutiny take place? *(on a ship)* What was the gag rule? *(The rule in Congress forbidding any discussion of antislavery petitions.)*

Reading Skills
Using Text Organization

Explain that chronological order is used to tell the incredible story of Cinque's capture and the events leading to the *Amistad* incident. Have partners use the text to list the events in order, using complete sentences.
ANALYZING

Skills Connection
Geography

Using a classroom world map or the map on pages 214-215, have students locate Sierra Leone on the west coast of Africa, trace a route from there to Havana, Cuba, and the route from Havana to Connecticut.

TEACHING CHAPTER 33
pages 177-179 1 class period, 35-50 minutes

Webster Defends the Union

In 1850, at great personal cost, Daniel Webster placed union before abolition in one last desperate compromise. Webster's sacrifice helped avoid war—but not for long.

ASK

1. What problem was created when California asked to enter the Union as a free state? *(In Congress, there would be more free states than slave states; if that occurred, the free states might pass a law forbidding slavery.)*
2. What were the main points of the Compromise of 1850 proposed by Henry Clay? *(California would be admitted to the Union as a free state; New Mexico and Utah would be territories; runaway slaves who reached free states would be returned to their owners; slaves couldn't be bought or sold in the nation's capital, though slavery would still be legal there.)*
3. Have students add information about the Compromise of 1850 to Resource 15 (TG Page 85).

DISCUSS

1. Why did Daniel Webster, who was against slavery, agree to the Compromise of 1850? *(He knew that the Union would fall apart if the free states didn't agree to it; the slave states in the South might secede from the Union if it was not passed; he would do anything to save the Union.)*
2. Why is making a compromise sometimes the best thing to do? *(Though no one wins everything they want, everyone at least gets something. And everyone involved can move on—not be stuck in the argument.)*

WRITE

Have students choose one senator—Henry Clay, John C. Calhoun, or Daniel Webster. They should write a brief paragraph telling the senator's position on the Compromise of 1850 and describe something about the man.

Ponder
Have you ever compromised? Was it the right thing to do? Was there a time when you *should* have compromised?

Question Chart

LITERACY LINKS

Words to Discuss

compromise   nullify
confederacy   Unionist
fugitive slave law secession

Work with students to define each term from context. Then ask partners to create a Venn diagram with the headings *Unionist* and *Secessionist*. To begin, have students write *Compromise of 1850* in the intersecting circles. Then ask students to put each vocabulary term in the diagram, and add other words from the chapter that belong.

Reading Skills
Identifying Rhetorical Devices

Explain that great speechmakers try to persuade their audiences by appealing both to emotions and to reason. Help students analyze Webster's speech on page 179. ANALYZING

- What words does he repeat to reinforce his points? *(secession; peaceable secession; No, sir!)*
- What emotionally loaded words does he use? *(distress, anguish, miracle)*
- What images does he use? *("as the snows on the mountain melt" "as I see the sun in heaven")*

Meeting Individual Needs
English Language Learners

Students may encounter several unfamiliar words in the chapter. Help them to understand the vocabulary under Words to Discuss, and encourage them to use the dictionary and context clues. You may wish to pair students with advanced readers to help their understanding.

PART 7 | 57

TEACHING CHAPTER 34 pages 180-185 1 class period, 35-50 minutes

Big Problems and a Little Giant

Senator Stephen Douglas saw popular sovereignty as the key to his political and financial future. His defense of the Kansas-Nebraska Act resulted in bloodshed in the West over slavery.

ASK

1. Why did Stephen Douglas introduce the Kansas-Nebraska Act? *(to win Southern votes to build a transcontinental railroad across a northern route)*
2. What did the Kansas-Nebraska Act say about slavery? *(the people in the territories would have the right to decide for themselves whether to allow slavery)*
3. What was the end result in Kansas of the Kansas-Nebraska Act? *(warfare between pro-slavery people and anti-slavery people)*

Ponder
Stephen Douglas made a hasty decision that he was sorry for later. Has that ever happened to you?

Question Chart

DISCUSS

1. How did the idea of popular sovereignty turn into a problem that Douglas had not considered? *(Pro-slavery and anti-slavery forces rushed to the territories to try to sway the elections to their side. This caused bloodshed and destroyed any hope of compromise.)*
2. Reread with students "A Compromise, Not a Solution" on page 62. Ask: How did the Kansas-Nebraska Act undo the Missouri Compromise of 1820? *(The Missouri Compromise said that, apart from Missouri, the rest of the territory from the Louisiana Purchase north of 36°30' would be free territory. The Kansas-Nebraska Act repealed the Missouri Compromise, allowing residents of the remaining territories to decide whether they wanted slavery.)*
3. Have students add information about the Missouri Compromise and the Kansas-Nebraska Act to Resource 15 (TG page 85).

WRITE

Ask students to suppose they are reporting the incident in the Senate when Preston Brooks attacked Charles Sumner. Have them write a newspaper article for a Washington, D.C. newspaper describing the scene.

LITERACY LINKS

Words to Discuss

repealed   free soiler
popular sovereignty
border ruffian

Have students agree on a definition for *popular sovereignty*. *("people power," or the right of the people to decide for themselves)* Have students look up the meaning of *ruffian* and *repealed* in the dictionary. Ask: Which phrase describes a Kansas abolitionist? *(free soiler)* Which describes a pro-slavery supporter in Kansas? *(border ruffian)*

Reading Skills
Understanding Cause and Effect

Have partners make a cause-effect chart for the Kansas-Nebraska Act. Have them keep in mind questions such as "Why did it happen?" (to find a cause) and "What happened as a result?" (to find an effect).
SYNTHESIZING

- Why did Douglas introduce the Kansas-Nebraska Act? *(to win Southern votes for a railroad in the North)*
- What happened as a result of Brooks's attack on Sumner? *(John Brown killed pro-slavery people.)*

Skills Connection
Geography

Have students examine the map on page 182 and cross-reference it with the map on pages 216-217. Have them determine which present-day states, or parts of states, were included in the Kansas and Nebraska territories in 1854. *(Kansas Territory: present-day state of Kansas and part of Colorado. Nebraska Territory: present-day state of Nebraska, much of South Dakota, North Dakota, Wyoming, and most of Montana.)*

58 | LIBERTY FOR ALL?

TEACHING CHAPTER 35   pages 186-187   1 class period, 35-50 minutes

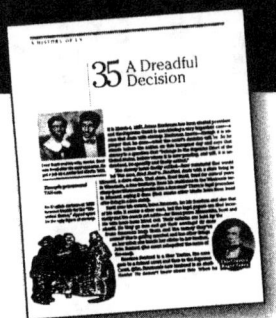

A Dreadful Decision

The Dred Scott decision declared that enslaved Africans were property. This decision crushed hopes for a peaceful resolution to the slavery issue.

ASK

1. Who was Dred Scott? *(a slave)* Where did he live and why was it important? *(He was living in Missouri, a slave state, but had lived in Wisconsin, a free territory.)*
2. Why, with the help of abolitionist John Sanford, did Dred Scott go to the Missouri courts? *(to ask for his freedom because he had lived in a free state)* What happened? *(The Missouri court said that Scott, who it declared wasn't a free citizen, was not entitled to go to court.)*
3. What was the decision in the Dred Scott case? *(Scott lost.)* What did U.S. Chief Justice Roger Taney say about the Missouri Compromise? *(It was unconstitutional since it prevented slave owners from taking their property to the territories.)*

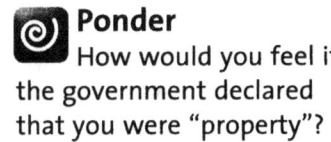

Ponder
How would you feel if the government declared that you were "property"?

Question Chart

DISCUSS

1. What did Chief Justice Taney mean when he said that slaves were "protected" by the Fifth Amendment? *(Slaves were property and the Fifth Amendment protects property.)* What did that mean for Dred Scott and other slaves? *(As property, slaves had no rights.)*
2. Have students add information to Resource 15 (TG page 85).
3. Dred Scott had gone to court to try to win his freedom several times. What kind of person do you think he must have been? *(Responses will vary.)*

WRITE

Ask students to reread the caption for the handbill on page 187. Then, on a large sheet of paper, have them write a handbill of their own that announces a meeting about the Dred Scott decision. The handbill should express an opinion about the case.

LITERACY LINKS

Words to Discuss

majority opinion
dissenting opinion

Help students define the words from context. Then ask partners to use the dictionary to help them make a word web for *dissent* (verb). Have them include related words, such as *dissent* (noun), *dissenter*, *dissension* and the antonym *assent*.

Reading Skills
Analyzing a Cartoon

Help students analyze the political cartoon on page 186. ANALYZING

- Who are the figures? *(a slave; two figures, probably meant to represent the South and the North)*
- What is the man tearing? *(a map of the U.S.)*
- What is the message of the cartoonist? *(Slavery is ripping apart the U.S.)*

Skills Connection
Geography

Have students use the maps on pages 182 and 216-217 to help reinforce their understanding that Missouri became a slave state under the Missouri Compromise of 1820 and that the Wisconsin territory was free.

PART 7 | 59

TEACHING CHAPTER 36
pages 188-190 — 1 class period, 35-50 minutes

Fleeing to Freedom

Ellen and William Craft took an amazing freedom journey to flee bondage in the South. They joined other fugitive slaves on the lecture platform to prove that slavery was anything but a "positive good."

ASK

1. Why did the black slave Ellen Craft look like a white woman? *(Her mother was a black slave owned by her father, who was white.)*
2. What happened to Ellen when she was 11 years old? *(She was given as a wedding present to her white half-sister.)*
3. How did Ellen and William Craft escape to freedom? *(Ellen dressed up as William Johnson, an ill male white slave owner taking his slave North.)*
4. What did the Crafts do after they reached the North? *(They became famous for speaking out for abolition and for telling the story of their escape.)*

Ponder
How difficult do you think it would be to travel to a new land where you did not speak the language or have any friends?

✓ Question Chart

DISCUSS

1. Why do you think the Crafts took a big risk in speaking out publicly for abolition? *(Slave catchers wanted to catch them and take them back to the South.)*
2. Why do you think slave owners would especially want to have the Crafts captured? *(They wouldn't want slaves to be encouraged by the Crafts' example or to have such popular people speaking out for abolition.)*

WRITE

Ask students to write a news article for the abolitionist paper *The Liberator* describing how Ellen Craft smuggled her husband out of Georgia.

L I T E R A C Y   L I N K S

Words to Discuss

biracial

Explain that the prefix *bi-* means "two." *Biracial* means "two races." Point out that being biracial is not limited to people who are part black and part white. Discuss that people may be multi-racial, or descended from more than two races.

Reading Skills
Analyzing Graphic Aids

Have students study the Sale of Slaves and Stock advertisement on page 190. Encourage them to use the chart to make inferences about the the life expectancy of slaves on Georgia plantations in 1852 *(only 4 of the slaves are over 47 years old, suggesting a short life expectancy)* and the kind of work slaves did *(field work, housework, cook, blacksmith, nursemaid)* Ask: What work seemed to be most highly valued? *(rice and cotton workers)*
INFERRING

Meeting Individual Needs
Auditory Learners

The story of Ellen Craft and her freedom journey is a good opportunity to have students practice reading aloud. Ask volunteers to read a paragraph as students follow along in their books. Pause after each paragraph to ask questions to determine learners' understanding and to provide opportunity for questions.

60 | LIBERTY FOR ALL?

TEACHING CHAPTER 37
pages 191-195 • 1 class period, 35-50 minutes

Over the River and Underground

Both black and white Americans organized a "freedom train" to the North. The Underground Railroad was fueled by the desire of slaves for freedom and the commitment of individual Americans to liberty.

ASK

1. What was the Underground Railroad? *(a network of secret escape routes and helpers that enabled enslaved blacks to reach freedom)*
2. Why were the citizens of the college town of Oberlin, Ohio, put on trial? *(They rescued the slave John Price, who had been kidnapped from Oberlin by slave catchers, and put him on a train to Canada.)*
3. Why was it illegal to be part of the Underground Railroad? *(It violated the Fugitive Slave Law.)*
4. Why were the Oberlin Trials big news? *(They placed the Fugitive Slave Law on trial; showed willingness of some people to violate the law, if necessary, to end slavery.)*

Ponder
Do you know people who are as brave and courageous as the conductors on the Underground Railroad?

Question Chart

DISCUSS

1. Direct students to the feature Driving that Train on page 195. How do you think the conductors of the Underground Railroad managed to keep their communications secret? *(When they wrote letters or spoke in public places about their activities, they spoke as if they were really talking about a railroad; for example by referring to the enslaved peoples as "stock" and of "forwarding" stock, meaning getting slaves to the next safe "depot.")*
2. Being a conductor on the Underground Railroad was a form of civil disobedience or passive resistance. What might Henry David Thoreau have thought of the conductors? *(He would have approved of their methods and thought they were brave.)*

WRITE

Have students write a paragraph describing the basic way that the Underground Railroad operated. Encourage them to use the terms used by the people who ran the Railroad.

LITERACY LINKS

Words to Discuss

station   conductor
passenger
Underground Railroad

Have students use context to make sure they understand the meaning of the vocabulary. Then ask them to make a visual aid of the Underground Railroad, labeled with these terms.

Reading Skills
Using Graphic Aids

Have students study the map on page 193 and answer these questions.
ANALYZING

- Where did some people go to escape slavery? *(Canada, Nova Scotia, Bahamas, Mexico, Cuba)*
- What cities were stations on the Underground Railroad? *(Detroit, Jonesboro, Boston, and so on)*
- Were there more stations along the Northern routes or the Southern routes? *(Northern routes)*

Meeting Individual Needs
Visual Learners

Ask volunteers to analyze the illustration on page 192 and connect their observations to the information in the text. You may wish to prompt their comments by asking questions such as: Who do you think the white people are? Which people are getting out of he cart? What are they carrying? Where do you think they came from? Does the place seem to be in the North or the South? Why? What time of day does it seem to be?

PART 7 | 61

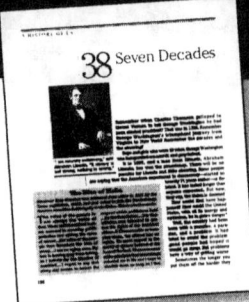

TEACHING CHAPTER 38
pages 196-198   1 class period, 35-50 minutes

Seven Decades

The crisis over slavery presented American democracy with its greatest test. Whether the Union survived—and realized its ideals of liberty and equality—rested upon finding a way to end slavery. The solution would come at the point of a gun.

ASK

1. Who was elected President in 1860? *(Abraham Lincoln)* What are the words that follow this quote from Lincoln: "If slavery is not wrong, . . . " *("nothing is wrong.")*
2. According to the author, what was America's promise, paradox, and problem? *(Promise: the words of the Declaration of Independence. Paradox: in the land of equality and liberty, slavery was permitted. Problem: finding a way to solve the injustice of slavery.)*
3. What would it take to end the problem? *(civil war and three amendments to the Constitution)*
4. Which groups, besides African Americans, did not have equal rights? *(Native Americans, Asians, and women and children)*

Ponder
What do you think the country's Founders would have said about the United States in 1860?

 **Question Chart**

DISCUSS

1. Reread with students the feature A Stand for Peace on page 197. Ask: How could Douglass be against the Mexican War and for the Civil War? *(He believed the Mexican War was unjust, and was fought to gain territory from Mexico and was supported by people who wanted to bring slavery to that territory, but that the Civil War was just, since it was fought to give slaves their liberty.)*
2. What were some of the bills and decisions that fueled the struggle between abolitionists and pro-slavery people? *(Missouri Compromise, Compromise of 1850, Kansas-Nebraska Act, Dred Scott decision, Fugitive Slave Law)*

WRITE

Ask students to neatly transcribe the words from the Declaration of Independence reproduced on page 197. Challenge interested students to memorize the words, and to recite them in a choral reading.

LITERACY LINKS

Words to Discuss

paradox   **unalienable**

Have students use context or a dictionary to define the terms, and then write sentences using them. Point out that *paradox* is a statement or condition that contains a contradiction.

Reading Skills
Understanding Word Choice

Point out the metaphor "When it [civil war] was over, America's childhood was over." Ask: What does the author mean by saying America's childhood was over after the war? *(America was no longer innocent: its people had gone to war with each other. It had faced the worst of times and had grown mature.)* ANALYZING

Skills Connection
History/Economy

Remind students that the invention of the cotton gin sparked the growth of slavery. Have students consider whether, if similar technological advances had been made in planting and harvesting cotton, slavery might have ended. Or was slavery already too much a part of the Southern life style?

62 | LIBERTY FOR ALL?

SUMMARIZING PART 7

THINKING ABOUT THE THEMES

The following questions will help students relate the book's themes to the content of Part 7. You may wish to use these questions for classroom discussion or have students answer them in written form.

1. What was the major conflict in the United States in 1860? *(whether slavery would be ended or the Union would be dissolved)*
2. What was the position of the Unionists? *(Unionists wanted to preserve the Union, and didn't want some of the states to secede.)*
3. What did the Dred Scott decision say about the human rights of enslaved peoples? *(Slaves were property, and so had no rights.)*
4. Draw students' attention to the other themes that have been posted around the room. Give them the opportunity to explore the relevance of these themes to Part 7. Accept choices that are supported by sound reasoning.

ASSESSING PART 7

Use Check-Up 7 (TG page 70) to assess student learning.

NOTE FROM JOY HAKIM

How do you teach about right and wrong? Through stories—the stories of heroines, heroes, and villains. People may get away with misbehaving in the short run, but hardly anyone escapes the judgment of history.

PROJECTS AND ACTIVITIES

▶ Reporting the News

Have the class work in groups to write newspaper editorials about the events in Kansas after the Kansas-Nebraska Act was passed. Ask volunteers to read their editorials aloud.

▶ Abolitionist Posters

Have students work in groups to design and illustrate posters that abolitionists might have created to advertise an appearance by Ellen and William Craft, a discussion of the Dred Scott decision, or a meeting of Free Soilers. Review with students the meaning of loaded words, or words that pack an emotional wallop. Tell them to use at least three loaded words on their posters.

▶ Dialogue on the Underground Railroad

Have two groups each write and perform dialogues between abolitionists and escaped slaves on the Underground Railroad. Dialogues should include real place names and describe routes on the network.

▶ Song

Have students write a poem, a rap, or the lyrics for a song about Cinque and the *Amistad* passengers. Students should include several historical facts in their writing. Encourage student volunteers to perform their songs for the class.

★★ FACTS TO SHARE ★★

In 1977 a group of African Americans hung a plaque on the St. Louis courtroom where the Dred Scott trials were first held. The plaque read: "Dred Scott: American, Pioneer, participant in the legal struggle for citizenship that rocked America."

Check-Up 1

Answering these questions will help you understand and remember what you have read in Chapters 1-7. Write your answers on a separate sheet of paper.

1. Imagine that you are each of these key figures. You want to ensure that future generations remember your role in history. For each person, complete this statement: "I am important to the expansion of the United States because I . . ."
   a. Thomas Jefferson
   b. Jedediah Smith
   c. Zebulon Pike
   d. William Becknell
   e. Brigham Young

2. Describe each of these locations. Then explain why each was important to westward expansion.
   a. Great American Desert
   b. South Pass
   c. Beckwourth Pass
   d. Santa Fe

3. Compare and contrast the reasons people followed these trails west.
   a. Oregon Trail
   b. Mormon Trail
   c. Santa Fe Trail

4. What was the significance of towns such as St. Louis, Missouri, and Council Bluffs, Iowa?

5. Why did people on wagon trains draw up contracts?

6. How was the New Mexico Territory acquired by the United States, and from whom? Who was living in New Mexico at that time?

7. Between 1847 and 1854, 1.6 million Irish people came to America. Why did most of them leave Ireland?

8. Suppose you wanted to head to California in 1849. You have read reports about the conditions along each overland route. Which route would you choose? Why?

9. Why was each of these places significant to Mormons?
   a. Palmyra, New York
   b. Nauvoo, Illinois
   c. Great Salt Lake

10. Use the graph and information from your reading to answer the questions.
    a. Why did so few pioneers travel the Oregon Trail in 1843?
    b. In what year did the most people travel to Oregon on the Oregon Trail? About how many took the trip that year?
    c. The 1860 U.S. Census showed that Oregon had 52,456 residents. What do the totals on this graph tell you about where most of these people came from?

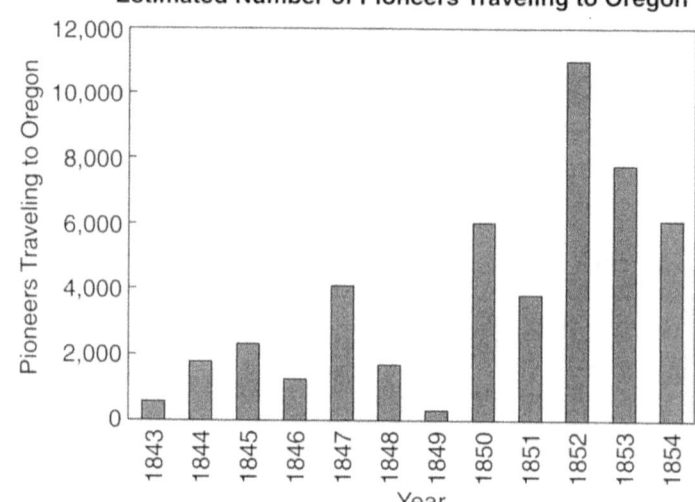

Estimated Number of Pioneers Traveling to Oregon

Name _____ Date _____

Check-Up 2

Answering these questions will help you understand and remember what you have read in Chapters 8-12. Write your answers on a separate sheet of paper.

1. What roles did the following people play in the westward expansion of the United States?
   a. James K. Polk
   b. John Frémont
   c. Richard Dana
   d. James Marshall

2. Who lived in a Spanish mission? What was the purpose of a mission, and what activities took place there?

3. Define *manifest destiny*. How did belief in manifest destiny affect American westward expansion?

4. What significant contributions did the following people make to the history of Texas?
   a. Stephen Austin
   b. Davy Crockett
   c. Sam Houston

5. What was the importance of the Rio Grande in the war between Mexico and the United States?

6. What did Abraham Lincoln, Henry Clay, and Frederick Douglass think about President Polk and his belief in manifest destiny?

7. Why was slavery a major issue when Texas applied for statehood?

8. What was significant about the timing of the signing of the Treaty of Guadalupe Hidalgo and the discovery of gold at Sutter's mill?

9. What was nativism? How did nativism affect the Chinese in California? Whom did the nativists attack on the East Coast?

10. Indicate the location of these lands acquired by the United States. Label the map with the corresponding letters.
    a. Texas, 1836
    b. Land disputed between United States and Mexico, 1845-1848
    c. Mexican Cession, 1848

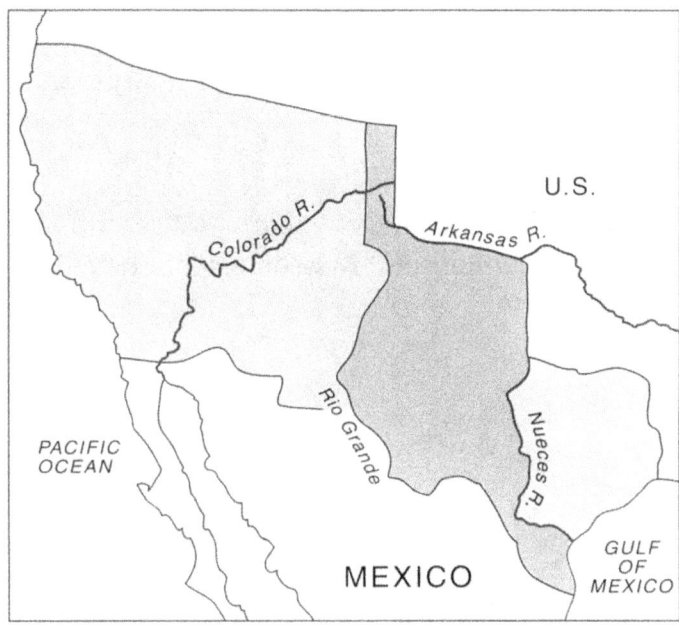

CHECK-UP 2 | **65**

Check-Up 3

Answering these questions will help you understand and remember what you have read in Chapters 13-17. Write your answers on a separate sheet of paper.

1. These people played key roles in events described in Chapters 13-17. Tell who each person was and what he did of importance during this period.
   a. Samuel F. B. Morse
   b. Nathaniel Bowditch
   c. John Manjiro
   d. Prince Boston

2. What did pigeons, horses, and electricity have to do with communication in the mid-1800s?

3. Why was the Pony Express started? How did it work? What brought about its end?

4. How were clipper ships and stagecoaches important to the expansion of the United States?

5. What did the cities of Salem, Massachusetts, and New Bedford, Massachusetts, have in common?

6. Explain the meaning of each of the following terms:
   a. Yankee
   b. "Thar she blows!"
   c. Nantucket sleigh ride
   d. baleen

7. What were some of the products made from whales? How did kerosene affect the whaling industry?

8. In the 1800s, the form of government in Japan was feudalism. How did this differ from government in the United States?

9. What did Commodore Matthew Perry's mission to Japan accomplish? What role did Nakahama Manjiro play in this?

10. What do you think was the most important advance of this time in communications and in transportation? Write a paragraph naming each advance. Support your opinion with details from the textbook.

Check-Up 4

Answering these questions will help you understand and remember what you have read in Chapters 18-20. Write your answers on a separate sheet of paper.

1. These people played key roles in the events described in Chapters 18-20. Tell who each person was and what he did that was important.
   a. John Deere
   b. Cyrus McCormick
   c. Elias Howe
   d. Horace Greeley
   e. John Jacob Astor

2. Explain how each of these places is connected to progress in the United States between 1820 and 1860.
   a. Astor House Hotel
   b. Stewart's Department Store
   c. Rock Island, Illinois

3. How did technology and new inventions change cities?

4. What problems did fast-growing cities face?

5. What caused conflict in the Northwest Territory?

6. How did neighbors in the Northwest Territory help each other?

7. The crossing of the Mississippi River by a Chicago and Rock Island train in 1856 was a major event. Explain the effects of this event on the following:
   a. Midwestern farmers
   b. steamboat companies
   c. relations between North and South

8. Choose one person from this period whom you admire. Tell why you feel this way.

9. Horace Greeley wrote these famous words in a newspaper: "Go west, young man." How did Americans at this time feel about heading for the frontier?

10. Use the graph to answer these questions.
    a. What were the percentages of urban and rural residents in 1790?
    b. What were the percentages of urban and rural residents in 1860?
    c. What trend in the United States does this graph illustrate?

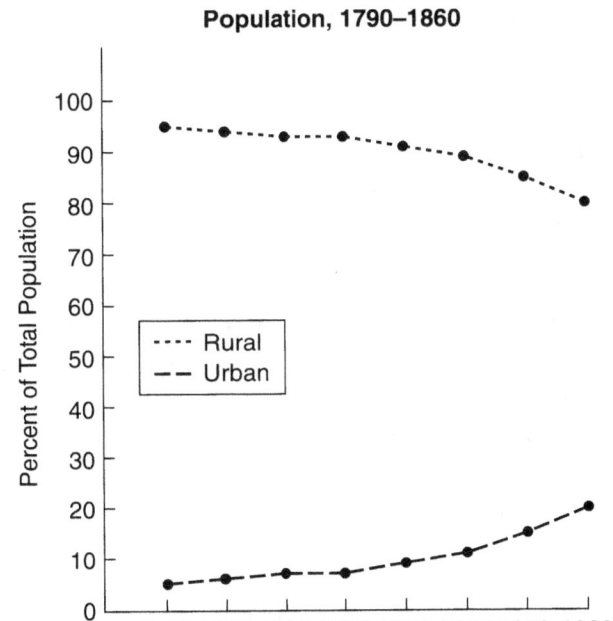

U.S. Rural and Urban Population, 1790–1860

CHECK-UP 4 | 67

Name _____   Date _____

Check-Up 5

Answering these questions will help you understand and remember what you have read in Chapters 21-26. Write your answers on a separate sheet of paper.

1. These people played key roles in the events described in Chapters 21-26. Tell who each person was and what she did that was important.
   a. Elizabeth Cady Stanton
   b. Elizabeth Blackwell
   c. Dorothea Dix
   d. Susan B. Anthony

2. Imagine you are a member of a national historical society. You have to place historical markers at each of these sites. Write two or three sentences for each place describing its importance to the expansion of the rights of American people.
   a. Litchfield Female Academy
   b. Mount Holyoke
   c. Seneca Falls, New York
   d. Oberlin College

3. Horace Mann believed that democracy depended on good free public schools. Do you agree? Why?

4. Define each of these terms. Then explain how each term relates to the expansion of human rights.
   a. universal education
   b. abolitionist
   c. labor union

5. What rights were demanded by the women who attended the Seneca Falls Convention? How did they change the words of the Declaration of Independence to make their point?

6. What were the main points made by Sojourner Truth in her "A'n't I a Woman?" speech? Why did she make the speech?

7. Describe the working conditions in the Lowell mills.

8. Whom among the reformers from this period do you admire? Write a brief paragraph explaining your choice.

9. What issues did Rebecca Harding bring to people's attention in her novel *Life in the Iron Mills*?

10. Indicate the year of these important events in the reform movement on the timeline. Label the timeline with the corresponding letters.
    a. Seneca Falls Convention
    b. Sojourner Truth's "A'n't I a Woman?" speech
    c. Shoemakers' strike in Lynn, Massachusetts
    d. Mount Holyoke College founded
    e. Strikes declared legal by Massachusetts Supreme Court
    f. Dorothea Dix begins crusade to aid mentally ill

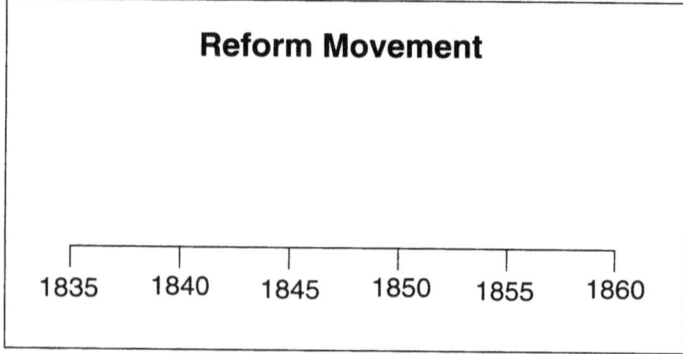

68 | CHECK-UP 5

Name _____ Date _____

Check-Up 6

Answering these questions will help you understand and remember what you have read in Chapters 27-31. Write your answers on a separate sheet of paper.

1. These individuals were important in the events described in Chapters 27-31. What did each person do?
   a. George Ticknor
   b. Ralph Waldo Emerson
   c. Louisa May Alcott
   d. Herman Melville
   e. James Fenimore Cooper

2. In what way did these places play a part in the story of American literature from 1830 to 1850?
   a. New England
   b. Walden Pond
   c. New York

3. Which of Henry David Thoreau's ideas inspired twentieth-century leaders Mohandas Gandhi and Dr. Martin Luther King, Jr.? Explain these ideas.

4. Thoreau was against the decision to go to war with Mexico. What did he do to express his disagreement?

5. Tall tales became an American specialty. What are the elements of a tall tale?

6. What were the subjects of George Catlin's and John Audubon's paintings? Why did they hurry to paint their subjects?

7. Of 1,800 poems written, only eight were published during this poet's lifetime. Who was this poet? What made this writer's work different from most poetry of the time?

8. "Beat! beat! drums!—blow! bugles! blow! / Through the windows—through doors—burst like a ruthless force, / Into the solemn church, and scatter the congregation. . . ." Who wrote these lines? What is the poet talking about?

9. Why does the author call Walt Whitman "the poet of democracy"?

10. Complete the chart by checking the home region of each writer.

Writer	New York	New England
Henry David Thoreau		
James Fenimore Cooper		
Louisa May Alcott		
Henry Wadsworth Longfellow		
Herman Melville		
Washington Irving		
Ralph Waldo Emerson		
Emily Dickinson		
Walt Whitman		
Nathaniel Hawthorne		

Name _____ Date _____

Check-Up 7

Answering these questions will help you understand and remember what you have read in Chapters 32-38. Write your answers on a separate sheet of paper.

1. These people were involved in the conflict over slavery. How did each influence that struggle?
   a. John C. Calhoun
   b. Henry Clay
   c. Stephen Douglas
   d. border ruffians and Free Soilers
   e. John Brown

2. The Compromise of 1850 held the nation together. What in the compromise pleased the North? What in the compromise pleased the South?

3. The Compromise of 1850 resulted from the work of Henry Clay, John Calhoun, and Daniel Webster. What were the goals of each of these senators?

4. What does *popular sovereignty* mean?

5. Explain how Kansas became known as "Bleeding Kansas."

6. Who was Frederick Douglass? What was his role in the struggle against slavery?

7. What was the purpose of the Underground Railroad? Explain how it worked.

8. How did the Dred Scott decision affect the rights of black Americans?

9. How did these trials help to divide the nation?
   a. *Amistad* trials
   b. Oberlin trials

10. Indicate the year of these important events in the struggle over slavery on the timeline. Label the timeline with the corresponding letters.
    a. Lincoln elected president
    b. Dred Scott case
    c. "Bleeding Kansas"
    d. Oberlin trials
    e. Kansas-Nebraska Act

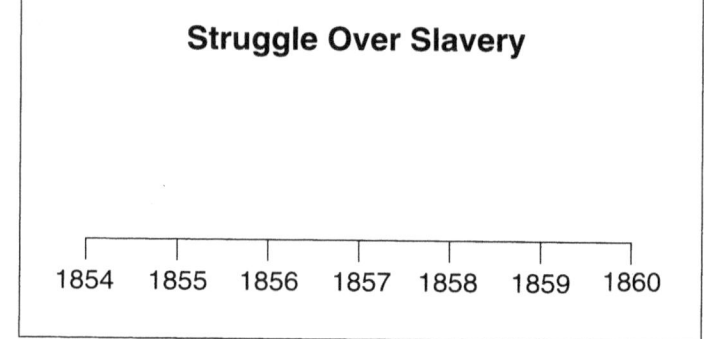

Struggle Over Slavery

1854 1855 1856 1857 1858 1859 1860

70 | CHECK-UP 7

Name _____   Date _____

Resource 1

QUESTION CHART: *LIBERTY FOR ALL?*

★ What were the major events?

★ Who were the significant people?

★ What were the important ideas?

Name _____ Date _____

Resource 2

TERRITORIAL EXPANSION OF THE UNITED STATES, 1783-1853

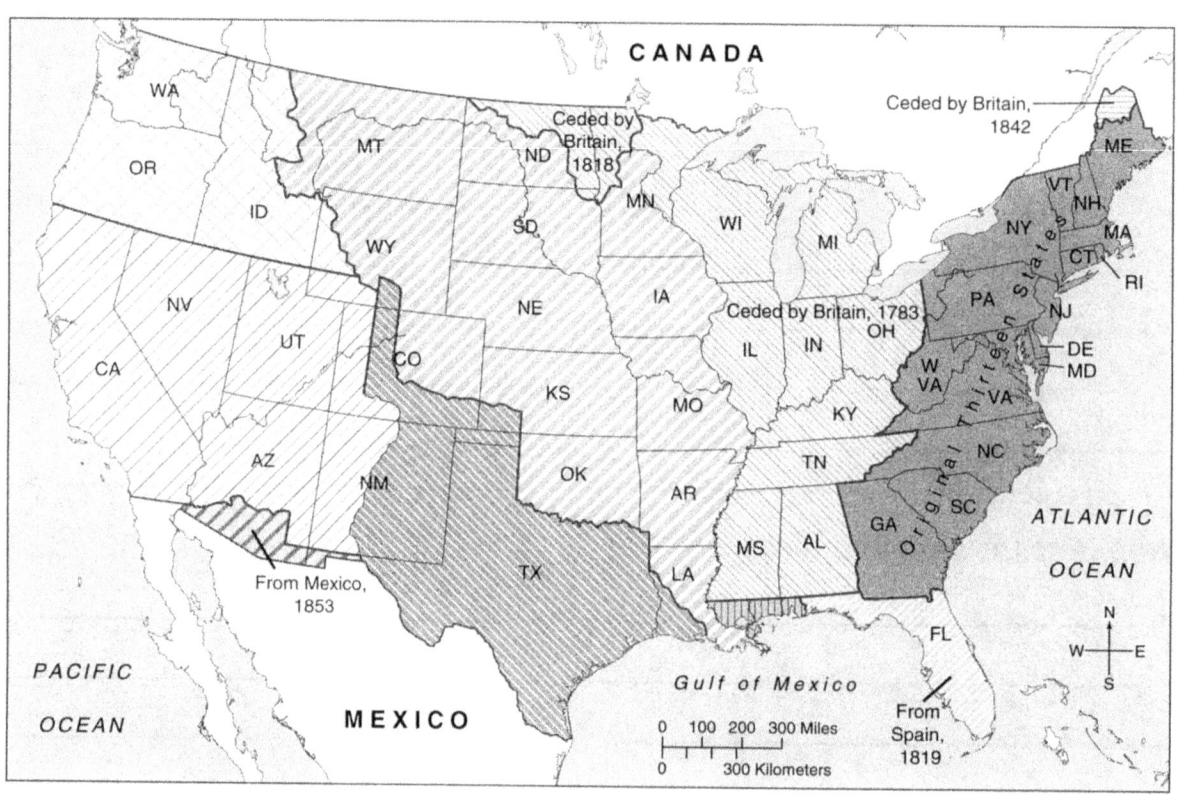

1. On the map, use these names and dates to label each expansion of the United States.
   a. Louisiana Purchase, 1803
   b. Texas Annexation, 1845
   c. Oregon Country, 1846
   d. Mexican Cession, 1848

2. Write the name of each state that was fully or partially included in each of the following expansions:
   a. Louisiana Purchase _____

   b. Texas Annexation _____

   c. Oregon Country _____

   d. Mexican Cession _____

Name _____ Date _____

Resource 3

TRAILS WEST

Directions Identify and label each of the following trails on the map: *Santa Fe Trail, Oregon Trail, California Trail, Mormon Trail*. Then read the excerpts from *Liberty for All?* and identify the trail each group of pioneers traveled.

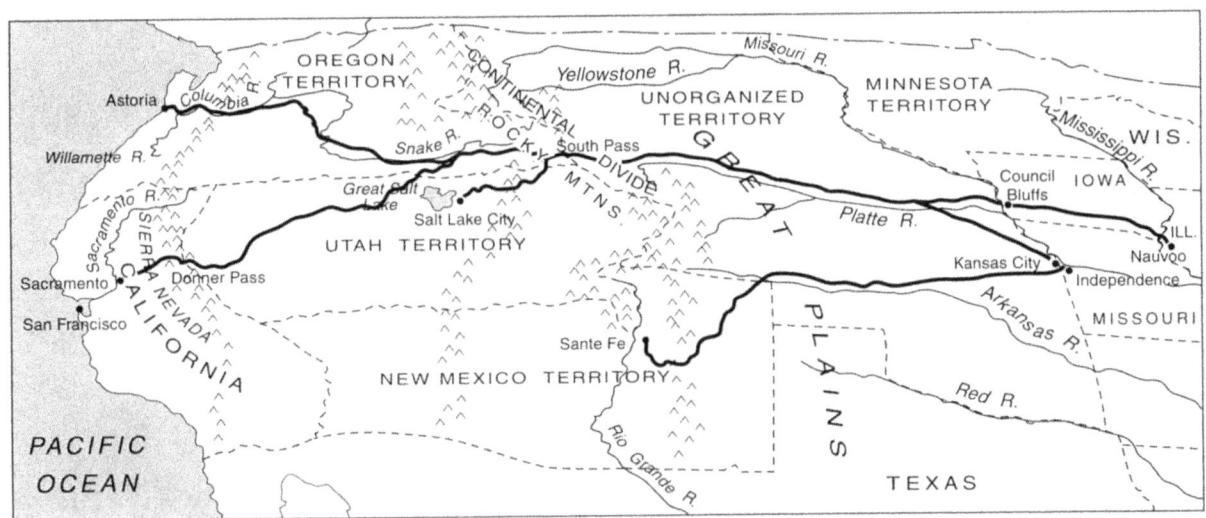

1. "They didn't plan to settle. . . . Their heavy wagons were pulled by teams of mules or oxen and were filled with cotton cloth, tin cups, socks, mirrors, cutlery, ribbons, buttons, glassware, ink, hats, gloves, and silk shawls."

   _____

2. "But Brigham Young planned well. . . . Young sent groups ahead to create stopping places, build shelters, plant crops, mark the trail, prepare for the wagon trains."

   _____

3. "You come down from the Rockies in high spirits. The Utah desert discourages you a bit, but the Humboldt River with its grassy banks cheers you again."

   _____

4. "It must have looked like an enormous parade—with wagons, cattle, chickens, dogs—and more than 1,000 pioneers. (About 600 of them were children.)"

   _____

Name _____ Date _____

Resource 4

GOLD RUSH TRUE-OR-FALSE

Directions   For each statement about the California gold rush, write *True* or *False* on the line. If the statement is false, make it true by crossing out the incorrect detail and writing the correct detail above.

_____ 1. Gold was discovered by John Sutter in 1848 when he was building a mill.

_____ 2. California became a United States territory nine days after gold was discovered.

_____ 3. Most forty-niners came overland from the East because it was the fastest route.

_____ 4. In 1849, about 80,000 gold seekers arrived in California.

_____ 5. Mining was hard work, and few miners became wealthy.

_____ 6. Miners came from all over the world.

_____ 7. The population of San Francisco swelled from 812 to 250,000 in only two years.

_____ 8. The people who were most likely to become rich during the gold rush were government employees.

_____ 9. Prices of goods in California skyrocketed because there was too much supply for the demand.

_____ 10. Capitalists led attacks on Chinese immigrants in California.

_____ 11. Gold and silver were discovered in the Appalachian Mountains as well as in California.

_____ 12. Enough people stayed in California for it to become a state quickly.

Name _____ Date _____

Resource 5

A BIOGRAPHICAL PROFILE

Directions Use this chart to take notes about an important figure in the fight for Texas independence. Find information in your textbook and another source to complete the chart. Then write a two- or three-paragraph biographical profile of the person. Include the important events of his life, how the person affected Texas independence, and what happened to the person after independence.

When and Where Born	
Early Life	
Skills or Jobs	
Political Career	
Military Career	
Personality Traits	
When and Where Died	

RESOURCE 5 | **75**

Name _____ Date _____

Resource 6

THE CONCORD STAGECOACH

The Concord stagecoach was a popular type of coach in the 1800s for travel between cities and in the West. They were built by J. Stephens Abbot and Lewis Downing in their factory in Concord, New Hampshire. The coaches were built high off the ground with a wide body, so that they could handle the rough roads of the young country. The frame of the body curved outward slightly, giving it strength and a little more space for the passengers. The coaches could carry up to eighteen passengers: nine packed inside and nine perched on top.

The Concord coaches pioneered a new form of suspension. Instead of steel springs, the coach body rested on leather *thoroughbraces*, which were strips of thick steerhide. This caused the stagecoach to have a rocking motion once it got up to speed. In his book *Roughing It*, Mark Twain called the Concord "an imposing cradle on wheels." Each coach weighed about 2,500 pounds and cost $1,100.

Directions Read the definitions of the parts of the stagecoach. Then label the diagram with the names of the parts.

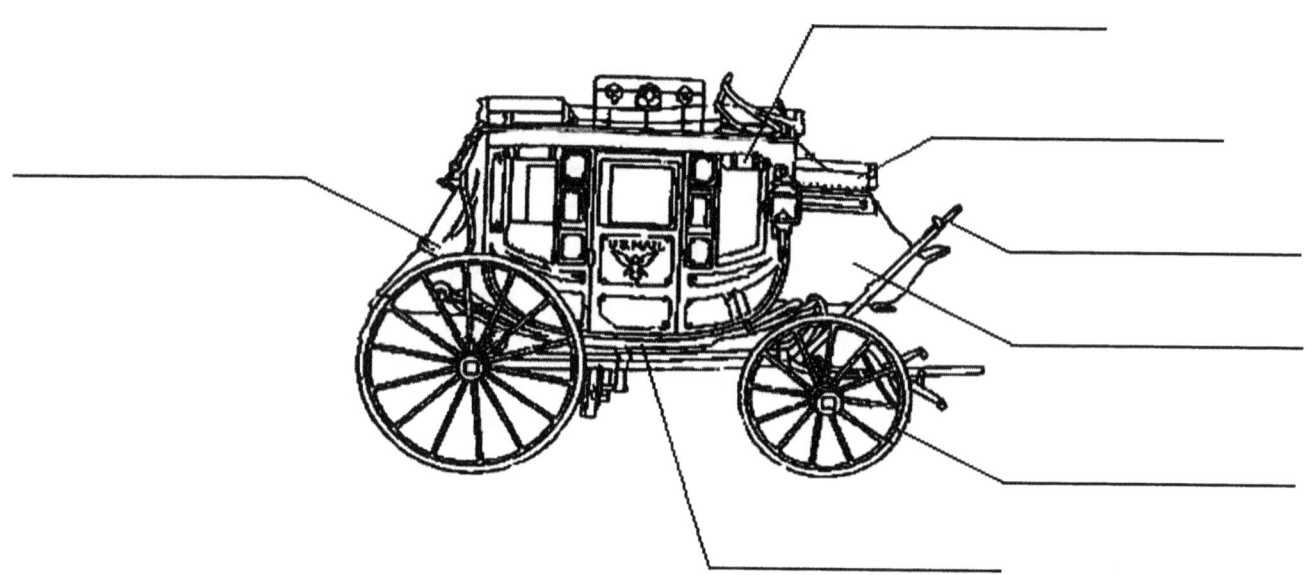

Driver's box Seat for the driver. The driver was the *whip*. The guard was the *shotgun*.
Curtains Curtains on the open windows protected passengers from mud, dust, and weather.
Front boot Leather storage compartment under driver's box for valuable items, such as gold and silver shipments.
Hand brake Handle that driver pulled to slow the coach and keep it from hitting the horses.
Wheel Hub was made of seasoned elm, spokes of tough oak, rim of hardy hickory.
Thoroughbraces Strips of leather running beneath the coach body from front to back. They supported the body and softened the bounces of the ride.
Rear boot Leather storage compartment in back for luggage and other packages.

Name _____ Date _____

Resource 7

URBAN POPULATION EXPLOSION

A line graph is one way to show how something changes over time. Usually, the years being studied are written along the bottom of the graph, while the numbers for the subject being studied are written up the side of the graph.

Directions Use the data in the table to make a line graph showing the population growth of New York and Cincinnati from 1820 to 1860. Then answer the questions.

1. Round each number for New York to the nearest ten thousand.

2. On the line graph, use a ruler to help you find the point matching each number to its year. Using one color pencil, mark each spot with a dot.

3. Using the same color pencil, draw a line connecting the dots. Color in the box for New York in the graph legend.

4. Using another color pencil, repeat Steps 1-3 for Cincinnati.

Population of New York and Cincinnati, 1820–1860

Year	New York	Cincinnati
1820	123,706	9,642
1830	202,589	24,831
1840	312,710	46,338
1850	515,547	115,434
1860	813,669	161,044

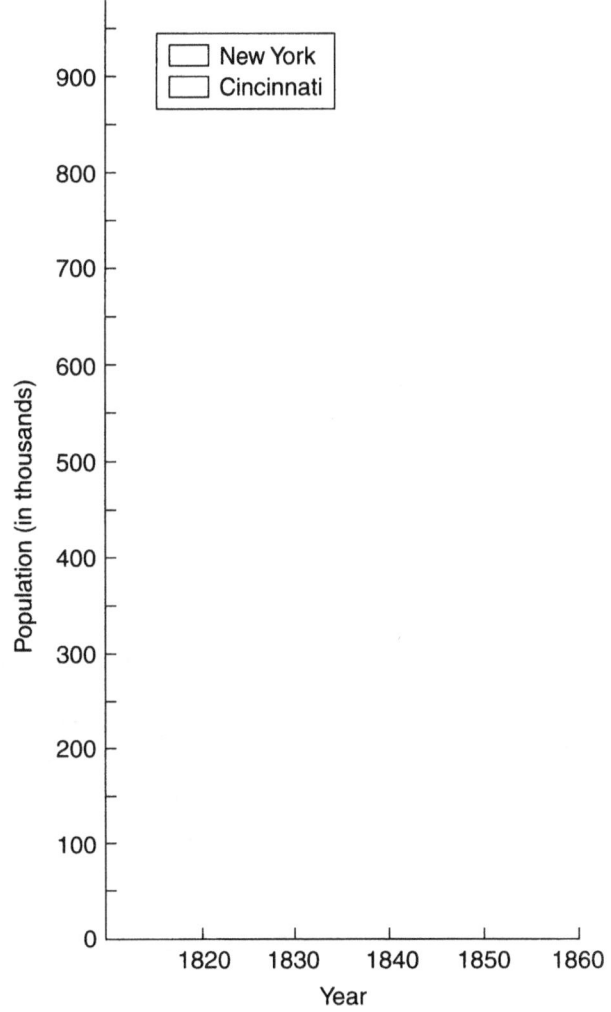

1. Use the table to find out how much each city's population increased between 1820 and 1860.

_____

2. Use the graph to find out in which decade each city's population grew fastest.

_____

Name _____ Date _____

Resource 8

CITIES AND WATERWAYS

Directions   The map shows the locations of the ten largest cities in the United States in 1860. Use the map to answer the questions.

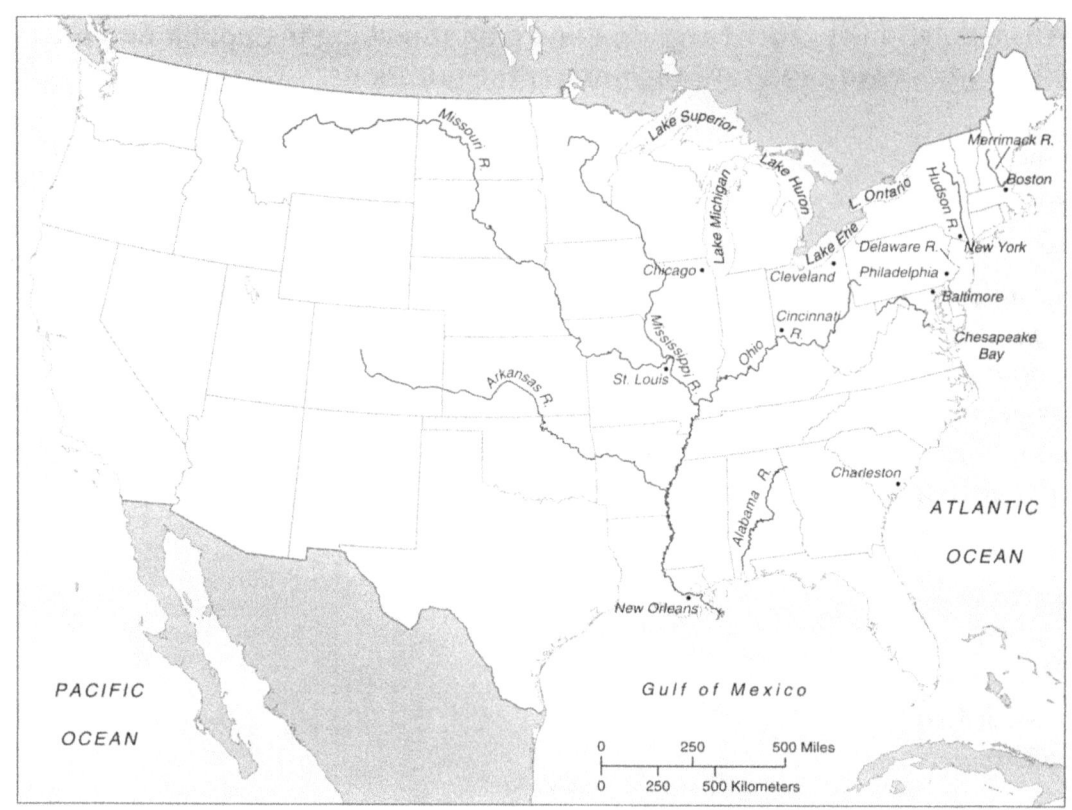

1. Identify the body (or bodies) of water near which each city is located.

Baltimore _____   Cleveland _____
Boston _____   New Orleans _____
Charleston _____   New York _____
Chicago _____   Philadelphia _____
Cincinnati _____   St. Louis _____

2. Why are the largest cities located on major bodies of water?

_____

_____

3. Imagine you are a farmer living near Cincinnati in 1860. Describe the route that your products might take to get to markets in the East.

_____

_____

78 | RESOURCE 8

Name _____ Date _____

Resource 9

MCGUFFEY'S READER

William McGuffey's *Readers* were first published in 1836, and they were the country's most widely used textbooks for 75 years. They were used to teach reading, pronunciation, grammar, and comprehension. The stories were often taken from the Bible, or involved fables and other stories that taught manners and morals. Following is Lesson 52 from the *New Fourth Eclectic Reader: Instructive Lessons for the Young* (1866).

Directions Read the lesson. Then, on a separate sheet of paper, answer the questions from the original lesson.

EMULATION

Pronounce correctly. Do not say *speakin* for speak-ing; *recollec* for rec-ol-lect; *evinin* for e-ven-ing; *frienship* for friend-ship; *wider* for wid-ow; *gain* for gained; *seein* for see-ing.

1. Frank's father was speaking to a friend, one day, on the subject of competition at school. He said that he could answer for it, that envy is not always connected with it.

2. He had been excelled by many, but did not recollect ever having felt envious of his successful rivals; "nor did my winning many a prize from my friend Birch," said he, "ever lessen his friendship for me."

3. In support of the truth of this, a friend who was present, related an anecdote which had fallen under his own notice, in a school in his neighborhood.

4. At this school, the sons of several wealthy farmers, and others, who were poorer, received instruction. Frank listened with great attention, while the gentleman gave the following account of the two rivals.

5. It happened that the son of a rich farmer, and of a poor widow, came in competition for the head of their class. They were so nearly equal, that the teacher could scarcely decide between them; some days one, and some days the other, gained the head of the class. It was determined, by seeing who should be at the head of the class for the greater number of days in the week.

6. The widow's son, by the last day's trial, gained the victory, and kept his place the following week, till the school was dismissed for the holidays.

7. When they met again, the widow's son did not appear, and the farmer's son being next to him, might now have been at the head of his class. Instead of seizing the vacant place, however, he went to the widow's house, to inquire what could be the cause of her son's absence.

8. Poverty was the cause; she found that she was not able, with her utmost efforts, to continue to pay for his tuition and books, and the poor boy had returned to labor for her support.

9. The farmer's son, out of the allowance of pocket-money, which his father gave him, bought all the necessary books, and paid for the tuition of his rival. He also permitted him to be brought back again to the head of his class, where he continued for some time, at the expense of his generous rival.

Exercises. What is the subject of this lesson? What do you mean by emulation? What is envy? What story is told about the two rivals? Is it right to envy a classmate who has learned his lessons better than yourself?

Name _____ Date _____

Resource 10

WORKERS' WAGES, HOURS, AND EXPENSES

Directions Use the data in the Wages and Hours and Weekly Budget tables to calculate the missing averages in the chart below. Then answer the questions.

Wages and Hours, 1840s		
Job	Weekly Wage	Daily Hours
Dressmaker	$1.50	15
Vegetable peddler	$4.00	12
Teamster	$6.00	12
Female mill worker	$2.25 and board	13
Male mill worker	$6.00	12
Mill supervisor	$12.00	12

Weekly Budget, New York City Family of Five, 1851	
Flour	$0.63
Sugar, butter, milk	1.09
Meat	1.40
Potatoes	0.50
Coffee and tea	0.25
Salt, pepper, cheese, eggs, etc.	0.40
Candles and fuel	0.54
Furniture and utensils	0.25
Rent	3.00
Clothing	2.20
Newspapers	0.12

Job	Weekly Wage	Hours/Day	Hours/Week (6 day week)	Earnings/Hour
Dressmaker	$1.50	15	90	less then $0.02
Vegetable peddler				
Teamster				
Female mill worker				
Male mill worker				
Mill supervisor				

1. Add up the total weekly expenses of a family of five in New York City in 1851. Write it on the following line. Which workers' wages could have supported the family?

_____

2. Given the wages, hours worked, and weekly expenses, how could a vegetable peddler's family make enough money to survive?

_____

_____

3. In 1850, travel from New York City to California cost several hundred dollars. Why do you think even more Easterners didn't try their luck in the gold fields?

_____

_____

Resource 11

WORKING IN THE LOWELL MILLS

Directions   This time table helps you understand what it was like to work in the textile mills of Lowell, Massachusetts in the 1850s. Use the information in the table to answer the questions.

TIME TABLE OF THE LOWELL MILLS,
To take effect on and after Oct. 21st, 1851.

The Standard time being that of the meridian of Lowell, as shown by the regulator clock of JOSEPH RAYNES, 43 Central Street

	From 1st to 10th inclusive.				From 11th to 20th inclusive.				From 21st to last day of month.			
	1stBell	2dBell	3dBell	Eve.Bell	1stBell	2dBell	3dBell	Eve.Bell	1stBell	2dBell	3dBell	Eve.Bell
January,	5.00	6.00	6.50	*7.30	5.00	6.00	6.50	*7.30	5.00	6.00	6.50	*7.30
February,	4.30	5.30	6.40	*7.30	4.30	5.30	6.25	*7.30	4.30	5.30	6.15	*7.30
March,	5.40	6.00		*7.30	5.20	5.40		*7.30	5.05	5.25		6.35
April,	4.45	5.05		6.45	4.30	4.50		6.55	4.30	4.50		7.00
May,	4.30	4.50		7.00	4.30	4.50		7.00	4.30	4.50		7.00
June,	"	"		"	"	"		"	"	"		"
July,	"	"		"	"	"		"	"	"		"
August,	"	"		"	"	"		"	"	"		"
September,	4.40	5.00		6.45	4.50	5.10		6.35	5.00	5.20		*7.30
October,	5.10	5.30		*7.30	5.20	5.40		*7.30	5.35	5.55		*7.30
November,	4.30	5.30	6.10	*7.30	4.30	5.30	6.20	*7.30	5.00	6.00	6.35	*7.30
December,	5.00	6.00	6.45	*7.30	5.00	6.00	6.50	*7.30	5.00	6.00	6.50	*7.30

* Excepting on Saturdays from Sept. 21st to March 20th inclusive, when it is rung at 30 minutes after sunset.

YARD GATES,
Will be opened at ringing of last morning bell, of meal bells, and of evening bells; and kept open Ten minutes.

MILL GATES.
Commence hoisting Mill Gates, Two minutes before commencing work.

WORK COMMENCES,
At Ten minutes after last morning bell, and at Ten minutes after bell which "rings in" from Meals.

BREAKFAST BELLS.
During March "Ring out"............at.......7.30 a. m................. "Ring in" at 8.05 a. m.
April 1st to Sept. 20th inclusive....at.......7.00 " "................. " " at 7.35 " "
Sept. 21st to Oct. 31st inclusive....at.......7.30 " "................. " " at 8.05 " "
Remainder of year work commences after Breakfast

DINNER BELLS.
"Ring out"......................12.30 p. m............."Ring in" .... 1.05 p. m.

In all cases, the *first* stroke of the bell is considered as marking the time.

1. According to the table, work begins at 10 minutes after the last bell in the morning. (In some months there are three morning bells; in others, only two.) Work continues until the evening bell. How long do the workers stay at the mill each day in January? In May?

_____

2. How much time do workers get to eat breakfast? Dinner? _____

3. In which months do workers start work before eating breakfast? _____

4. Suppose that your daily schedule were similar to that of the Lowell mill workers. When would you be able to do the other daily activities you need to do?

_____

Name _____   Date _____

Resource 12

AN AMERICAN LITERATURE

Directions   Use information from Chapters 27-30 to complete this graphic organizer comparing the American writers of the first half of the 19th century. In the left circle, list writers who mainly called New England home, and some details that apply only to them. In the right circle, do the same for the writers who mainly called New York home. In the section labeled *Both*, write a statement that refers to both groups of writers.

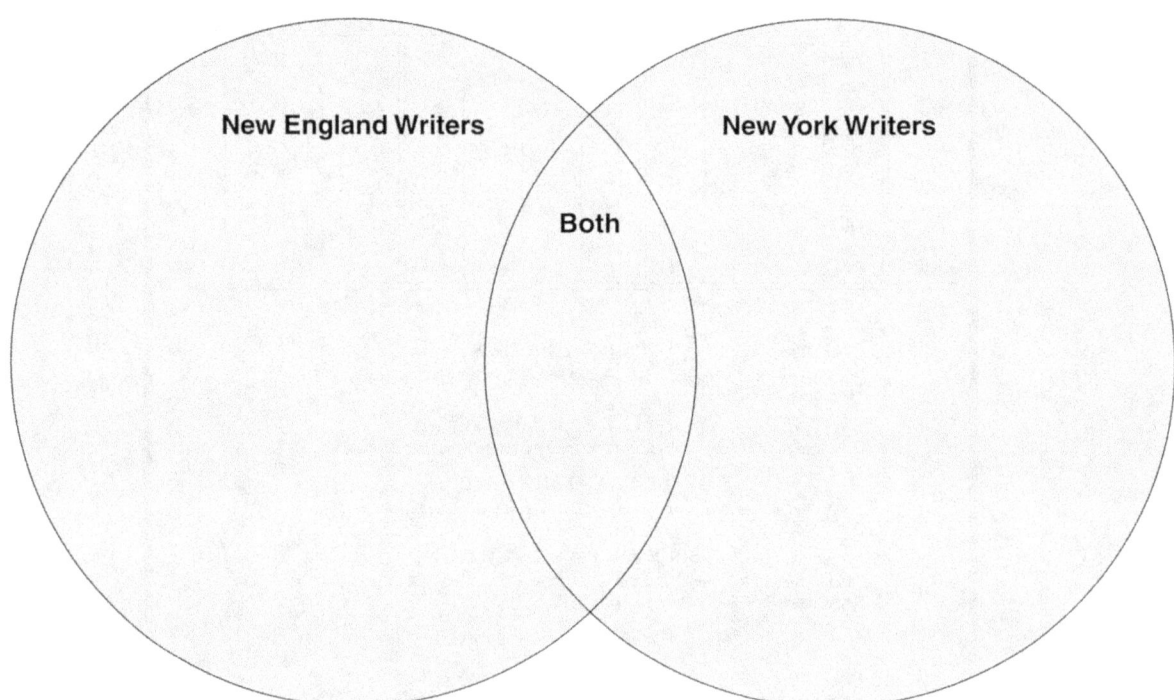

82 | RESOURCE 12

Resource 13

I HEAR AMERICA SINGING

Directions   Read the poem by Walt Whitman. Then answer the questions.

I Hear America Singing
I hear America singing, the varied carols I hear,
Those of mechanics, each one singing his as it should be blithe and strong,
The carpenter singing his as he measures his plank or beam,
The mason singing his as he makes ready for work, or leaves off work,
The boatman singing what belongs to him in his boat, the deckhand
   singing on the steamboat deck,
The shoemaker singing as he sits on his bench, the hatter singing as he stands,
The wood-cutter's song, the ploughboy's on his way in the morning, or
   at noon intermission or at sundown,
The delicious singing of the mother, or of the young wife at work, or of
   the girl sewing or washing,
Each singing what belongs to him or her and to none else,
The day what belongs to the day—at night the party of young fellows,
   robust, friendly,
Singing with open mouths their strong melodious songs.

1. A *symbol* is a word that stands for something else. In this poem, what do you think *singing* is a symbol for?

2. What jobs does Whitman mention?

3. How does the poet express that each person is important?

4. What idea about the American people do you get from Whitman's poem?

Name _____ Date _____

Resource 14

CONFLICT OVER SLAVERY: TIMELINE

Directions   Following are major events in the conflict over slavery in the first half of the 19th century. Match each event with a date on the timeline. Write the event in the appropriate box.

Foreign slave trade outlawed	"Four-Fifths" Compromise in Constitution	Compromise of 1850
Amistad mutiny	"Bleeding Kansas"	Oberlin trials
Missouri Compromise	Lincoln elected President	Kansas-Nebraska Act
Dred Scott decision		

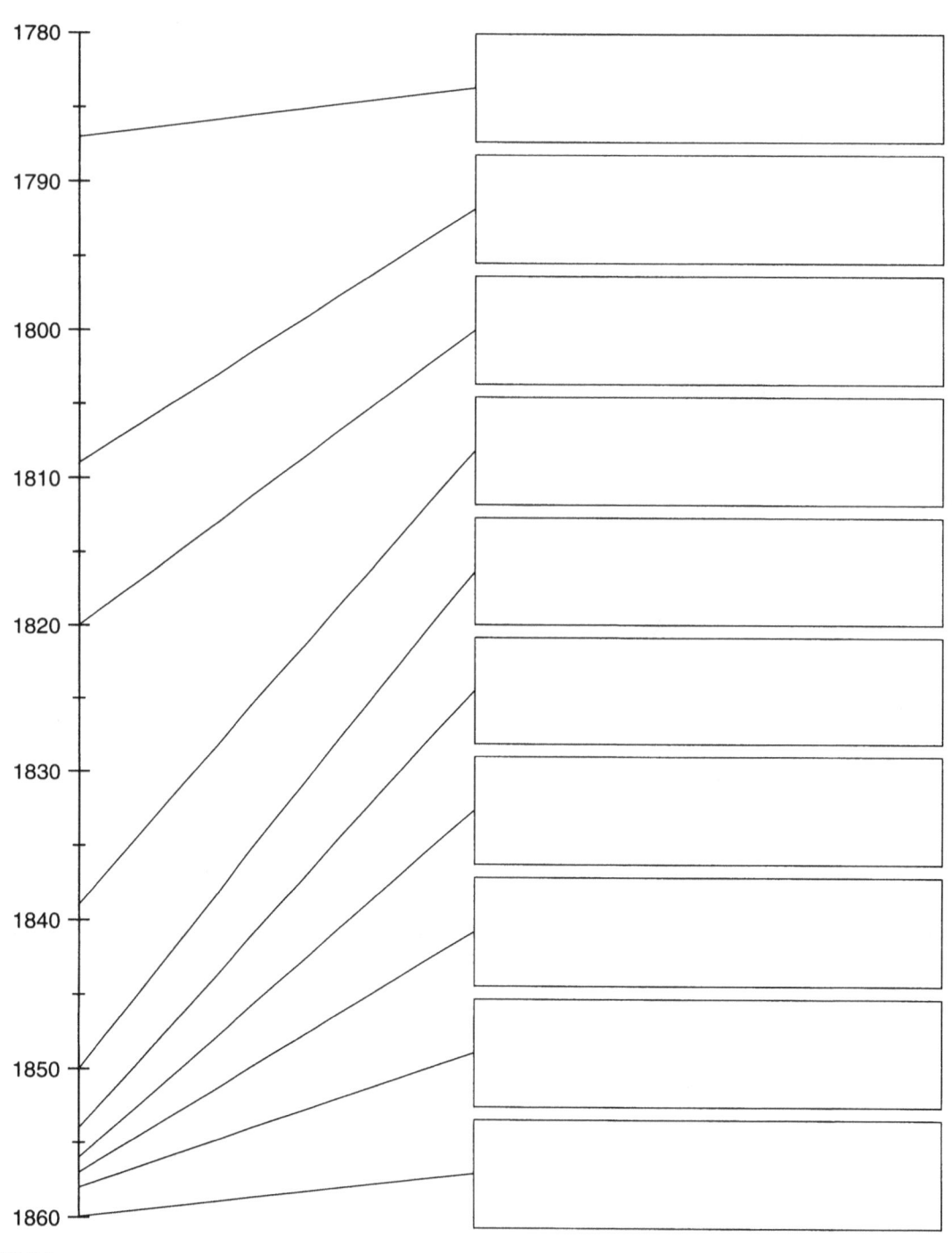

84 | RESOURCE 14

Name _____ Date _____

Resource 15

CONFLICT OVER SLAVERY: CONGRESS AND THE SUPREME COURT

Directions In the first half of the 19th century, the struggle over slavery began to tear the United States apart. Certain federal laws and Supreme Court decisions were extremely important in this struggle. Use information from Chapters 32-38 to complete the table summarizing the laws and Supreme Court decisions. Then answer the question.

Law or Decision	Major Points	Effects on Country
1. Missouri Compromise (1820)		
2. *Amistad* Decision (1841)		
3. Compromise of 1850		
4. Kansas-Nebraska Act (1854)		
5. *Dred Scott* Decision (1857)		

6. Compare the feelings in the nation about slavery before the Missouri Compromise with those feelings after the Kansas-Nebraska Act.

_____

_____

RESOURCE 15 | 85

ANSWER KEY

CHECK-UP 1

1. (a) President of the U.S., bought Louisiana Territory from France (b) mountain man who explored the west to California and discovered South Pass (c) explored Southwest, discovered Pikes Peak (d) opened Santa Fe Trail, beginning trade with Mexico (e) Mormon leader; settled Utah territory
2. (a) Name for the Great Plains; thought to be uninhabitable, so pioneers kept going to Oregon. (b) a gap in the Rocky Mountains through which the pioneers traveled on their way west (c) pass through Sierra Nevada to California (d) New Mexico town; destination for traders like Josiah Gregg
3. (a) Pioneers wanted land, the opportunity to make money, a new life, and to escape the depression. (b) Mormons were escaping religious persecution and wanted to go to an uninhabited land where they could be free. (c) Traders wanted to trade goods with the Mexicans in Santa Fe.
4. They were jumping-off towns for the pioneers; places where pioneers bought supplies, teamed up with other emigrants, and started out on the trails west.
5. Some wagon trains numbered many hundreds of people. The people drew up contracts to govern and organize their community.
6. New Mexico was part of Mexico and inhabited by Native Americans, Mexicans, and other Spanish-speaking peoples. James Magoffin convinced the governor of New Mexico not to resist the U.S. Army, which soon arrived and claimed New Mexico. There was no fighting.
7. There was a potato famine in Ireland.
8. Responses will vary. Students should use accurate geographic evidence to support their choices.
9. (a) Joseph Smith founded the Mormon religion and established a Mormon community. (b) City built by Mormons—the largest in Illinois. Mormons were persecuted and attacked by mobs that destroyed much of the city. (c) After the incidents at Nauvoo, followers of Brigham Young settled near the Great Salt Lake and quickly built a thriving community.
10. (a) That was the year the first wagon trains set out; people were unsure of going to Oregon that way. (b) 1852; 11,000 people (c) The bars on the graph add up to about 48,000 people; even assuming that some Oregon Trail travelers did not stay in Oregon or died along the way, most of the people in Oregon in 1860 arrived via the Oregon Trail.

CHECK-UP 2

1. (a) President who wanted California and Oregon (b) explorer who mapped much of the west, supported the Bear Flag republic in California, was senator from California, and ran for President (c) early visitor to California who wrote *Two Years Before the Mast*, which made people curious about California (d) carpenter who discovered gold on John Sutter's land, starting the California gold rush
2. Spanish priests, Indians; to teach Indians Christianity; agriculture, weaving, soap making, tanning, carpentry
3. Manifest destiny was the idea that Americans had the right and the duty to spread democracy across the continent; it supported the beliefs of settlers, President Polk, and others that it was their right to take over Texas and the Southwest from Mexico.
4. (a) Led a group of settlers to Texas from Missouri in 1821; more settlers followed, and by 1830 anglos outnumbered Mexicans. (b) Fought Santa Anna at the Alamo, a battle that inspired others to fight for Texas independence. (c) Texan leader who defeated Santa Anna at the Battle of San Jacinto; became president of the Republic of Texas.
5. The anglos believed that the southern border of Texas was the Rio Grande; Mexico disagreed. After the U.S. won the war, the border was established at the Rio Grande.
6. These people questioned Polk's motives for war with Mexico; they thought the war was more about gaining territory than about spreading ideals.
7. After its war for independence, Sam Houston supported the admission of Texas to the U.S. As a slave state, Texas would have upset the balance of power between slave states and free states in Congress. President Jackson said no. In 1845, under Polk, Texas became a state.
8. Nine days after gold was discovered in California, Mexico and the U.S. signed the treaty which gave California, the Southwest, as well as the disputed territories in Texas to the U.S. The forty niners were then free to go to California to seek their fortunes.
9. Nativism was the belief that only white Anglo-Saxon Protestants were "real" Americans. Nativists attacked the Chinese and passed laws that discriminated against the Chinese. They attacked Catholic immigrants from Europe on the East Coast.
10. (a) small area near Gulf of Mexico (b) area bounded by Rio Grande, Arkansas River, Nueces River (c) area from Rio Grande to Pacific Ocean

CHECK-UP 3

1. (a) painter and inventor of Morse Code and the telegraph (b) the "Arithmetic Sailor" who based calculations for longitude and latitude on mathematics and wrote a book about it that became a bestseller (c) translated Bowditch's system into Japanese, contributed to opening of Japan to America (d) patriarch of famous African American family in Massachusetts whose court case led to the Massachusetts Bill of Rights in 1780
2. Pigeons carried written messages; horses were used to send letters via the Pony Express and to carry mail on stagecoaches; electrical impulses carried Morse Code and messages from town to town.

3. to carry mail from Missouri as far as California; riders changed horses at stations 10 to 15 miles apart, about every 8 stations a new rider took over; stringing of telegraph wires across the continent

4. Clipper ships were fast ships that could take passengers and mail from Boston to San Francisco in 90 days; stagecoaches speedily took people and mail overland across the country. This lessened the time it took to travel from coast to coast, making expansion easier.

5. Both were rich port towns in New England; the towns were full of sailors and whalers; the people had contact with people and goods from all over the world.

6. (a) person from New England (b) the cry on a whaling ship when a whale was sighted (c) being dragged in a whaling boat by a whale after it has been harpooned (d) long plastic-like strips in the mouth of a right whale that filter plankton

7. Whale oil, candles, ambergris, buggy whips, corsets, decorative ivory objects. Kerosene gave a clearer light and had a better flame than whale oil; when kerosene became available, the demand for whale oil decreased.

8. In Japan, the feudal system kept people tightly restricted in classes from high class to low class. Everything was determined by a person's class. In the United States, democracy holds that all people have equal opportunity.

9. Perry made two voyages to Japan and convinced the shogun to open up trade to the United States. Manjiro had lived in the United States, spoke English, and had a private conversation with the shogun. After speaking with Manjiro, the shogun agreed to Perry's request.

10. Responses will vary, but should be supported by details from the text.

CHECK-UP 4

1. (a) invented steel plow (b) invented reaper (c) invented sewing machine (d) published New York Tribune; supported westward migration (e) created global trading network; richest man in America; helped develop New York City, founded some libraries

2. (a) hotel in New York that had running water in upstairs rooms (b) first department store (c) site of first bridge to span Mississippi River; carried a railroad across in 1856

3. Elevators made tall buildings possible, indoor plumbing brought convenience and better sanitation, newspapers allowed public to read the news. Growing industries brought new people to the cities, which increased the population.

4. crime, overcrowding, dirtiness, lack of sewers, disease, fire

5. Settlers were in conflict with Native Americans over land rights; blacks were sometimes kidnapped and enslaved; anti-slavery Quakers opposed those people who had slaves.

6. They worked together to clear land, cut logs, raise barns, quilt, husk corn, spin thread, and tend to the land; after working together, people held parties and danced and put on plays.

7. (a) Farmers gained a direct connection to the East Coast instead of sending goods down the Mississippi to New Orleans and up the Atlantic coast. (b) Steamboat companies would lose business to the railroads. (c) The North and South began to compete for Midwestern trade.

8. Responses will vary.

9. Americans most wanted land; they were willing to move from place to place, looking to pursue their dreams on the frontier.

10. (a) urban: 5 percent; rural: 95 percent (b) urban: 20 percent; rural: 80 percent (c) The country was becoming more urbanized.

CHECK-UP 5

1. (a) important leader at the Seneca Falls convention and in the women's suffrage movement (b) first woman to attend medical school in the U.S. (c) crusader for fair treatment of the mentally ill (d) important leader of women's suffrage movement; active abolitionist

2. Responses will vary, but should include these details: (a) early school for women that taught intellectual subjects, not just "women's subjects" such as needlework (b) one of the first women's colleges (c) site of the first women's rights convention in 1848 (d) college in Ohio that accepted women and blacks

3. Responses will vary. Students should note that for a democratic government to work, its citizens must be well informed and able to think for themselves.

4. (a) Education for all girls and boys; it acknowledged the rights of women to have an education; it gave all children the right to education. (b) A person who wanted to end slavery; abolitionists, who included many feminists and Quakers, spoke out against the injustices of slavery. (c) An organization of workers; unions fought for better conditions and the protection of workers.

5. The same rights given to men; they said, "We hold these truths to be self-evident, that all men *and women* are created equal."

6. She was as strong and tough as a man; she was strong enough to bear 13 children and see them sold as slaves. She opposed a man who said that women were weak and inferior to men.

7. The workers worked very long hours for little pay; the mills were very loud; the machines had many moving parts which caused accidents; the workers lived by a system of bells that regulated all their activities; young children worked extremely hard.

8. Responses will vary.

9. the dangerous, unhealthful conditions faced by the working people; their backbreaking work and the slave wages paid to them

10. (a) 1848 (b) 1851 (c) 1860 (d) 1837 (e) 1842 (f) 1843

CHECK-UP 6

1. (a) president of Harvard who encouraged students to write American literature (b) poet who was nicknamed the "Sage of Concord" and whose home was a meeting place for fellow writers (c) author of *Little Women* who supported her family and was the most popular author in the country (d) writer who worked as a whaler and afterward wrote *Moby Dick* (e) author of *Leatherstocking Tales*, the most popular adventure stories of the century
2. (a) Region where writers such as Hawthorne, Dickinson, Alcott, Emerson, and Poe lived. (b) Place where Henry David Thoreau wrote *Walden* in a house in the woods that he built himself. (c) Region where Whitman, Irving, Cooper, and Melville came from.
3. Gandhi and King were inspired by the ideas of civil disobedience (disobeying laws to protest something) and passive resistance (not fighting back when you are attacked, but not cooperating or running away or backing off, either).
4. He refused to pay his taxes and went to jail.
5. Tall tales are exaggerated stories about ordinary people who became heroes.
6. Catlin painted Native Americans in the West, Audubon painted birds and other wildlife. They were worried that their subjects would soon become extinct.
7. Emily Dickinson; she broke many of the rules of poetry regarding punctuation, rhythm, and rhyme.
8. Walt Whitman; the Civil War
9. Responses will vary, but students should note Whitman's emphasis on the American people in all of their diversity.
10. New York: Cooper, Melville, Irving, Whitman; New England: Thoreau, Alcott, Longfellow, Emerson, Dickinson, Hawthorne

CHECK-UP 7

1. (a) South Carolina senator who believed in states rights and called slavery a "positive good" (b) senator from Kentucky who introduced Compromise of 1850 (c) senator who introduced Kansas-Nebraska Act and wanted transcontinental railroad to run across the North (d) pro-slavery people from Missouri and anti-slavery settlers who battled for control of Kansas in 1856
2. North: California entered the Union as a free state; slaves could no longer be bought and sold in Washington, D.C. South: Runaway slaves who reached the North had to be returned to the South; slavery was still legal in Washington, D.C.
3. Clay wanted to keep the Union together as part-slave, part-free. Calhoun wanted the North to accept the legality of slavery. Although he was a bitter enemy of slavery, Webster wanted most of all to keep the Union together.
4. Popular sovereignty meant that voters in the western territories could decide for themselves whether they wanted to allow slavery there.
5. Because of popular sovereignty, pro-slavery and anti-slavery people rushed to Kansas so that their side could gain control. The two sides began fighting. The anti-slavery town of Lawrence was destroyed by pro-slavery people. John Brown killed five pro-slavery people.
6. Douglass was a former slave who had escaped from his master. He was a forceful writer and speaker in the cause of abolition.
7. The Underground Railroad was intended to help slaves escape to countries where slavery was not allowed and from which they would not be returned to their owners; people like Levi Coffin, who helped run it, found transportation and safe places for escaped slaves to stay on routes from the South to the North and Canada.
8. Blacks, either free or enslaved, had no right to citizenship.
9. (a) The Africans aboard the *Amistad* had killed white people, but they had been captured illegally and the slaver had broken English and Spanish law. The North supported freedom for the Africans; the South wanted them returned to Cuba and slavery. (b) The Oberlin trials were a test of the Fugitive Slave Law. Pro-slavery people wanted the Oberlin residents who freed John Price to be jailed for breaking that law. Anti-slavery people were furious at the government for jailing people for helping someone to become free.
10. (a) 1860 (b) 1857 (c) 1856 (d) 1858 (e) 1854

RESOURCE 1
Question Chart for use throughout the book.

RESOURCE 2
Maps should be labeled correctly.
1. Louisiana Purchase: Louisiana, Arkansas, Oklahoma, Missouri, Kansas, Nebraska, Iowa, Wyoming, South Dakota, North Dakota, Colorado, Minnesota, Montana
2. Texas Annexation: Texas, New Mexico, Kansas, Colorado, Wyoming
3. Oregon Country: Washington, Oregon, Montana, Idaho, Wyoming
4. Mexican Cession: California, Nevada, Utah, Arizona, New Mexico, Colorado, Wyoming

RESOURCE 3
Jumping-off points for the Oregon Trail were Independence, Missouri, and Council Bluffs, Iowa. The trail wound its way to Astoria in Oregon. The Mormon Trail and California Trail followed the route of the Oregon Trail for most of the way. The Mormons began their trek at Nauvoo, Illinois, and took the cutoff to the Great Salt Lake. California-bound pioneers took the southern route after they crossed the Continental Divide to get to Sacramento.
1. Santa Fe Trail 2. Mormon Trail 3. California Trail
4. Oregon Trail

RESOURCE 4
1. False; Gold was discovered by James Marshall.
2. True
3. False; Most forty-niners came overland because it was cheapest.
4. True
5. True
6. True
7. False; San Francisco's population swelled to 25,000 in only two years.
8. False; The people who were most likely to become rich were storekeepers.
9. False; Prices skyrocketed because there was too much demand for the supply.
10. False; Nativists led attacks on Chinese immigrants.
11. False: Gold and silver were also discovered in the Rocky Mountains.
12. True

RESOURCE 5
Students' charts should be completely filled out, and their biographical profiles should reflect the important details about their Texan's life. You may wish to have partners work on each personality.

RESOURCE 6
Clockwise from the left, the parts of the stagecoach should be labeled *Rear boot, Curtains, Driver's box, Hand brake, Front boot, Wheel, Thoroughbraces*.

RESOURCE 7
Line graphs should be completed accurately.
1. New York's population increased by 689,963 between 1820 and 1860. Cincinnati's population increased by 151,402 in the same period.
2. New York's population grew fastest between 1850 and 1860. Cincinnati's population grew fastest between 1840 and 1850.

RESOURCE 8
1. *New York, NY:* Hudson River, Atlantic Ocean; *Boston, MA:* Atlantic Ocean; *Philadelphia, PA:* Delaware River; *Baltimore, MD:* Chesapeake Bay; *Charleston, SC:* Atlantic Ocean; *Cincinnati, OH:* Ohio River; *Chicago, IL:* Lake Michigan; *Cleveland, OH:* Lake Erie; *St. Louis, MO:* Missouri River, Mississippi River; *New Orleans, LA:* Mississippi River, Gulf of Mexico
2. Water was essential for shipping goods and transporting people. Water also supplied power.
3. The farmer's products might be shipped down the Ohio River to the Mississippi River to New Orleans, and then along the Gulf Coast and up the Atlantic coastline to markets in the East.

RESOURCE 9
Students' responses will vary, but should be based on details in the excerpt.

RESOURCE 10
Data for chart—*Dressmaker:* $1.50, 15, 90, $0.02; *Vegetable peddler:* $4.00, 12, 72, $0.06; *Teamster:* $6.00, 12, 72, $0.08; *Female mill worker:* $2.25, 13, 78, $0.03; *Male mill worker:* $6.00, 12, 72, $0.08; *Mill supervisor:* $12.00, 12, 72, $0.17.
1. Only the mill supervisor could have supported a family of five.
2. The vegetable peddler's family would probably have gone to work. Perhaps the wife would have been a dressmaker and any children over eight or nine might have found work in a private workshop like the one shown on page 146 in the textbook. Together, a wife and three children might have earned six or seven dollars a week.
3. More Easterners did not go west because they barely had enough to feed themselves from day to day, let alone make a trip that cost several hundred dollars.

RESOURCE 11
1. January: from 6:50 A.M. (breakfast) until 7:30 P.M. (evening bell)—12 hours, 40 minutes; May: from 4:50 A.M. until 7:00 P.M. (evening bell)—14 hours, 10 minutes
2. 35 minutes for both breakfast and dinner
3. March through October
4. Responses will vary. There would be no time for sports, visiting friends, household chores, and so on.

RESOURCE 12
New England: Ralph Waldo Emerson, Richard Henry Dana, Henry David Thoreau, Francis Parkman, Nathaniel Hawthorne, Louisa May Alcott, Henry Wadsworth Longfellow, Emily Dickinson; many taught by George Ticknor at Harvard, leader was Emerson, the "Sage of Concord." *New York:* Herman Melville, James Fenimore Cooper, Washington Irving, Walt Whitman; adventure stories, American settings, frontier. *Both:* New American voices breaking from European influences, American subjects.

RESOURCE 13
1. *Singing* symbolizes each American's life and work.
2. mechanic, carpenter, mason, boatman, shoemaker, wood-cutter, mother, seamstress
3. Each person sings his or her own song, and they all seem to be equal in value.

4. The American people are a diverse group who all share in the optimistic, joyful spirit of the country. The country is made up of individuals enjoying a new kind of government and freedom.

RESOURCE 14
1787, "Four-Fifths" Compromise; 1808, Foreign slave trade outlawed; 1820, Missouri Compromise; 1839, *Amistad* mutiny; 1850, Compromise of 1850; 1854, Kansas-Nebraska Act; 1856, "Bleeding Kansas"; 1857, *Dred Scott* decision; 1858, Oberlin trials; 1860, Lincoln elected President.

RESOURCE 15
1. Missouri admitted as slave state, Maine as free state; no slavery in Louisiana Purchase north of 36°30', except in Missouri; Union is preserved, balance between free and slave states maintained.
2. Africans were enslaved illegally; they were freed. Abolitionists were cheered, pro-slavery people enraged.
3. California admitted as free state; New Mexico and Utah are made territories that can decide on slavery themselves; fugitive slave law will be enforced; slave trade cannot take place in Washington, D.C., but slavery is still legal there. Union preserved, but abolitionists enraged by fugitive slave law and possible extension of slavery into territories.
4. Creates Kansas and Nebraska territories, repeals Missouri Compromise, allows territories to decide on slavery (popular sovereignty). "Bleeding Kansas" (war and violence) results.
5. Blacks had no rights, slaves were property, Missouri Compromise was unconstitutional. Union splits more.
6. Possible response: Before the Missouri Compromise, there was hope that the country could exist half-free, half-slave. After the Kansas-Nebraska Act, the attitude became that the country could no longer exist half-free, half-slave, and that only war would decide the issue.

www.ingramcontent.com/pod-product-compliance
Lightning Source LLC
LaVergne TN
LVHW080250260326
834688LV00042BA/1212